WARBIRD
HISTORY

Messerschmitt 109

D. A. Lande

MBI Publishing Company

First published in 2000 by MBI Publishing Company,
729 Prospect Avenue, PO Box 1,
Osceola, WI 54020-0001 USA

MBI Publishing Company books are also available at
discounts in bulk quantity for industrial or sales-
promotional use. For details write to Special Sales
Manager at Motorbooks International Wholesalers &
Distributors, 729 Prospect Avenue, PO Box 1, Osceola,
WI 54020-0001 USA.

Edited by Michael Haenggi
Designed by Janis McKay Babcock

Library of Congress Cataloging-in-Publication Data
Lande, D. A.
    Messerschmitt 109 / D. A. Lande.
       p. cm. — (Warbird history)
    Includes bibliographical references and index.
    ISBN 0-7603-0803-9 (pbk. : alk. paper)
       1. Messerschmitt 109 (Fighter planes) 2. World
    War, 1939–1945—Aerial operations, German. I. Title.
    II. MBI Publishing Company warbird history.
UG1242.F5 L37   2000
623.7′464—dc21   00-058402

On the front cover: The nose-on view of an incoming
Messerschmitt Bf 109 was perhaps the worst sight
imaginable to Allied pilots trundling along in heavily-
laiden bombers headed to Berlin. Highly maneuverable
and loaded with guns, Bf 109s held a considerable
advantage over most aircraft in the sky. *John M. Dibbs*

On the back cover, top: A Bf 109F-5 thunders to life as its
crew tends to last-minute details before a reconnaissance
mission. The F-5 was essentially the same as the F-4, but
the engine-mounted cannon was removed and a camera
was fitted within the fuselage, just aft of the wings,
pointing directly downward. *Peter M. Bowers*
Bottom: A lone 109 waits silently on a grass strip for its
next mission. Its next call to duty could be breaking up
enemy bomber formations, escorting its comrades, or
taking on with the world's best fighters—all were part of
its repertoire. *Peter M. Bowers*

Printed in the United States of America

CONTENTS

	FOREWORD	5
	TRANSLATION NOTE	6
	ACKNOWLEDGMENTS	7
CHAPTER 1	BRAINCHILD OF AN AERONAUTIC GENIUS	8
CHAPTER 2	RAPID EVOLUTION	16
CHAPTER 3	COMBAT PROVING GROUNDS	30
	COLOR GALLERY	33
CHAPTER 4	BF 109s IN THE BATTLE OF BRITAIN	54
CHAPTER 5	PILOT TALK: GERMAN	64
CHAPTER 6	ADVANCED VERSIONS	70
CHAPTER 7	OVER SAND DUNES AND SNOW DRIFTS	86
CHAPTER 8	DEFENSE OF THE FATHERLAND	96
CHAPTER 9	PILOT TALK: BRITISH & AMERICAN	104
CHAPTER 10	TWILIGHT YEARS	112
	END NOTES	118
	BIBLIOGRAPHY	119
APPENDIX	SPECIFICATIONS	120
	SURVIVING AIRCRAFT	121
	INDEX	127

FOREWORD

From the E through K models, the Messerschmitt Bf 109 was my flying and fighting machine for more than five years. I developed an emotional and sentimental relationship with that plane. I flew her in the skies of France, England, the English Channel, the Balkans, the Mediterranean Sea, and Crete. I flew the F model, my personal favorite, in battle over the Crimean Peninsula, the Caucasus Mountains, Stalingrad, and Kursk. Finally, I flew the G model over Germany in home defense.

The 109 operated well under all weather extremes, including Russia's severe winters. We took off and landed in wind and on snow-covered surfaces. We cranked up the engine at temperatures as cold as -40 degrees Celcius, and had to pump kerosene into the lubrication line to liquify the freezing cold oil. The 109 flew through it all.

I learned the advantages the 109 had in combat and how to exploit them for greatest effect, as well as her disadvantages and how to avoid trouble because of them. I got to know all her idiosyncracies, as discussed in this book, such as the narrow undercarriage, the torque effect when the tail came up during takeoff, the effect of the slots in an abrupt tight turn, the tiny cockpit, and the poor visibility to the rear.

I also learned the capabilities and characteristics of my opponents in comparison. For instance, I found quickly that the 109 could not follow the Spitfire in a narrow climbing turn, and that the Thunderbolt was much faster in a dive and had a much higher structural strength. I flew all the other Luftwaffe fighters including, of course, the Fw 190. Comparing the two single-seat fighters is not easy. As weaponry, both were good, but in far different ways from each other. In a nutshell, I describe it this way: if the Fw 109 was a sabre, the 109 was a *florett*, or foil, like that used for the precision art of fencing.

This plane—a great design by Willy Messerschmitt—set a standard in aviation history and deserves an intense study and objective presentation of her technical design, her use and effect in combat operations, her pilots, and her charismatic presence. The 109 claims a place among the great and famous fighter planes of all time.

This book presents a great contribution to the Messerschmitt Bf 109's history.

Günther Rall

Günther Rall

Günther Rall is the highest scoring fighter pilot alive in the world today. He scored 275 confirmed victories during World War II, making him the third highest scoring fighter pilot of all time (following only the late Erich Hartmann and Gerhard Barkhorn, both also Bf 109 pilots). He survived eight bailouts, belly landings, and crashes; resulting injuries included repeated spine fractures that kept him hospitalized and out of the air contest for months. In postwar, he rose to the rank of lieutenant general and was appointed Chief of Staff of the German Air Force.

TRANSLATION NOTE

In this book, you'll see a variety of German terms pertinent to Messerschmitt Bf 109s. Most are not only German, but they carry unique meanings in the context of the Luftwaffe. For example, even the word *Luftwaffe* itself simply means "air weapon" in the German language. But it entails much more, of course, as the term we equate with the German Air Force.

We'll start with the most basic: In combat, Bf 109s flew in a fighter formation called a *Rotte*. This was the standard formation consisting of a pair of fighters—a leader and his wingman (called *Rottenhund* or *Rottenflieger*)—flying loosely together. Two *Rotte* combined to make a *Schwarm* of four aircraft. Typically, three *Schwarms* made a *Staffel*.

The *Staffel* was the smallest independent tactical unit in the Luftwaffe. Starting with the *Staffel*, here is an overview of the fighter structure, from smallest to largest:

German name	USAAF equivalent	Number of aircraft
Staffel	> 1/2 a Squadron	9 to 12
Gruppe	Squadron	30 (or slightly more)
Geschwader	Group	100 to 120
Fliegerkorps	Air Corps	250 to 500
Luftflotte	One air force	Varied

Geschwader and *Gruppe* were preceded by "*Jagd*" to indicate a single-engine fighter unit, e.g., *Jagdgeschwader*

(as opposed to a *Zerstörergeschwader*, which was a Bf 110 unit). *Jagdgeschwader*, the unit most commonly referred to, was abbreviated JG. *Jagdgeschwader* 3 was shortened to JG 3. The three (or more) *Gruppen*[2] within a *Jagdgeschwader* were denoted by Roman numerals placed in front of JG. For example, I/JG 3 would mean the first *Gruppe* of *Jagdgeschwader* 3. An Arabic number in front of JG specifies the *Staffel* within the *Jagdgeschwader*, such as 4./JG 3, which means the 4th *Staffel* of *Jagdgeschwader* 3.[3]

A *Staffel* was under the command of a *Staffelkapitan*—typically an *Oberleutnant* (USAAF first lieutenant equivalent) or *Hauptmann* (captain). A *Gruppe* was under the command of a *Hauptmann* or *Major* (major). A *Geschwader* was under the command of a *Major*, *Oberstleutnant* (lieutenant colonel), or *Oberst* (colonel).

Typically, a *Gruppe* occupied one airfield and functioned as an operational unit. Its three *Staffeln* were individual components that had their own heraldry, sometimes their own aircraft color scheme, and support personnel including the "black men"[4] or ground crew.

The *Geschwader* and smaller units were composed of aircraft of the same type. But in larger units, there was a mixture of aircraft. A *Fliegerkorps* had three or more *Geschwader* with a mixture of aircraft types. An integrated structure that combined different aircraft together made German units incomparable to the usually homogeneous USAAF or RAF units.

A *Luftflotte* had two or more *Fliegerkorps*. The largest tactical unit, a *Luftflotte* could be of a certain size and mix of aircraft according to the needs at hand.

ACKNOWLEDGMENTS

Special thanks to the many people who generously helped in this project. I couldn't have completed it without:

- Jonah Sielaff, whose youthful zeal for aviation motivated me and kept me smiling while I managed multiple projects.
- Peter M. Bowers, a godsend in the search for rare photos, including some from the archives of the late Heinz Nowarra.
- David Ethell, son of the late Jeffrey Ethell. He, along with his family, made me feel like an old friend.
- Nick Stroud, Aerospace Publishing Ltd., London. His can-do spirit helped put two excellent cutaway illustrations in this book for your perusal. Thanks also to Aerospace Publishing Ltd. for permission to include them.
- Brian Silcox, whose talent in aviation photography is manifested in his book, *The Best of the Past*, published by Mach 1, Inc.
- Mike Zimmerman, USAAF veteran of World War II and artist who painted *The Gustavs' First Pass*.
- Werner Oest, who willingly and humbly shared his wartime memories of Bf 109s. And his grandson Joe Vogler, who served as his masterful translator during an afternoon in Hamburg, Germany.
- Jack Ilfrey, who as an American fighter pilot, saw Bf 109s up close—so close that he collided with one over Berlin.
- Juha Pölkki, Embassy of Finland, Washington, D.C., for help in obtaining photos of Bf 109s in the Finnish Air Force.
- Ken Berner and Alice Schoening for help with photo reproduction.
- Susan Lurvey, staff librarian at the Experimental Aircraft Association.
- Dave Pfeiffer, researcher at National Archives.
- Brian Nicklas, researcher at the Smithsonian National Air and Space Museum.

I gratefully acknowledge the following publishers for permission to quote from their books: (any omissions are unintentional and will be corrected upon future printings). Heinz Knoke quotations are from his book, *I Flew for the Führer*, and are used with permission by Lionel Leventhal Publisher, Greenhill Books, London. Ulrich Steinhilper quotations are from his book, *Spitfire on My Tail*, coauthored with Peter Osborne, and are used with permission by Independent Books, 3 Leaves Green Crescent, Keston, Bromley, Kent BR2 6DN, England. J. E. Johnson quotations are from his book, *Wing Leader*, and are used with permission by Ballantine Books Inc., a division of Random House Inc., New York. Hans-Werner Lerche quotations are from his book, *Luftwaffe Test Pilot*, and are used with permission by Jane's Information Group Ltd., London. Adolf Galland quotations are from his book, *The First and the Last: The German Fighter Force in World War II*, and are used with permission of Methuen Publishing Limited. Jeffrey Quill quotations are from his book, *Spitfire: A Test Pilot's Story* (©1983, 1996 Jeffrey Quill) , and are used with permission by Crécy Publishing Limited. Douglas Bader quotations are from his book, *Fight for the Sky: The Story of the Spitfire and Hurricane*, and are used with permission by Sidgwick & Jackson, London. Willy Messerschmitt quotations are from Frank Vann's book, *Willy Messerschmitt*, and are used with permission by Patrick Stephens Limited, an imprint of Haynes Publishing, Sparkford, Nr Yeovil, Somerset, BA 22 7JJ, England. Beirne Lay quotations are from his article in the *Saturday Evening Post Anthology: Battle*, and are used with permission by Curtis Books, New York. The listing of surviving Bf 109s in the appendix is drawn from *Gallant Warriors Eighth Edition*, and is used with permission by Dennis Bergstrom. Quotations from Robert Olejnik, Jürgen Harder, and Richard Heemsoth in chapter 7 are from Armand van Ishoven's *Messerschmitt Bf 109 at War*, and are used with permission from Ian Allen Ltd., Hersham, England.

—D. A. Lande

CHAPTER 1

BRAINCHILD OF AN AERONAUTIC GENIUS

When the German Air Ministry called for a new fighter design to replace its aging fleet of Heinkel He 51 biplanes in 1934, German aircraft manufacturers scrambled to win the production contract. Specifications for the new first-line fighter were put into the hands of distinguished designers from three big-name manufacturers of the German aircraft industry: Heinkel, Arado, and Focke-Wulf. A young, somewhat obscure designer named Willy Messerschmitt was shunned from the competition.

Willy Messerschmitt had enjoyed limited recognition for innovation in civilian aircraft design, starting in the mid-1920s. He had attempted a few military aircraft designs, but had virtually *no* successful ones to his credit. Still, Messerschmitt was determined to enter the competition and show the world his ideas for an advanced design.

The best performing design won bragging rights—and a lucrative government contract that meant ongoing business for years to come. With Hitler's monstrous ambitions to resurrect and rearm his as-yet clandestine military, the value of the production contract went beyond anyone's wildest imagination at the time.

People in the German aircraft industry in the mid-1930s scoffed at the thought of Messerschmitt as a serious contender, let alone the man who would set the standard for all fighter aircraft to come in a world war. From the start, Messerschmitt's bid to win Germany's fighter contract seemed like a David versus Goliath struggle.

A Difficult and Clouded Reputation

Messerschmitt was an upstart, but to make matters worse, he wasn't an upstart who could enjoy the benefit of beginning with a clean slate. As a designer, he was not widely known, but what *was* known wasn't altogether good. Brash and supremely confident, even arrogant in the way of the prodigious, he wasn't well accepted among German aviators who knew him because of his strong and uncompromising assertions about the monoplane design. He was an ardent believer in the monoplane in a time when many were not yet willing to give up their standard, the biplane.

Worse still, Messerschmitt wasn't a complete unknown in the power circles of the German Air Ministry. In fact, he was *well* known to one particular man who, with the rising of Nazism, had reached a post second only to Air Minister Hermann Göring in the critical decision to choose the Luftwaffe's next-generation fighter. Messerschmitt's relationship with that man, Erhard Milch, Germany's new Reich Commissioner of Aviation, was anything but positive.

A new martial shape in the sky. Its design inspired by Willy Messerschmitt's *Taifun* (Typhoon), the Bf 109V-3 prototype soars over Bavaria in 1936. Powered by a 610-horsepower Jumo 210A engine, the aircraft could attain a speed of 395 miles per hour at 13,100 feet. This particular aircraft would be among the first three Bf 109s sent for testing under actual combat conditions in the Spanish Civil War. *Bowers Collection*

That story began in the late 1920s, when Messerschmitt himself was in his late 20s. By then, he had already founded a tiny aircraft design firm called Messerschmitt *Flugzeugbau*, and had walked away from that entrepreneurial venture to become chief designer of another small, but more established aircraft production company called BFW (Bayerische Flugzeugwerke).

Here, Messerschmitt designed an airliner for Deutsche Lufthansa, the national airline. Designated the M.20, the high-winged metal monoplane airliner had room for 8 to 10 passengers, or a payload of 2,200 pounds. Quite a heady accomplishment for a man not yet 30 and working mostly solo at that. But the launching of the M.20 design would be fraught with disaster that was to have far-reaching aftereffects for Messerschmitt.

On its maiden flight, February 26, 1928, the M.20 prototype met with grief. The pilot tried to bail out with a parachute at 250 feet and was killed. Sources conflict about the cause of the crash, but one theory is that the accident may have been averted had the pilot simply stayed at the controls: a minor ripping of fabric on the trailing edge of the mainplane likely caused the pilot to assume structural failure, and in the ensuing panic he abandoned the airplane needlessly.

Erhard Milch, exercising his authority as managing director of Lufthansa, deftly canceled the contract. However, when the second prototype flew safely in August, Milch reconsidered, then reinstated the original order for 10 M.20s. The next 2 M.20s were delivered in 1929. But before any others could be delivered, both crashed within a short time of each other. One was a grisly accident claiming the lives of eight *Reichswehr* officers—one of them a close personal friend of Milch. The cause of neither crash was conclusively determined.

Enraged, Milch held Messerschmitt personally responsible and was vocal in his criticisms. Newspapers across Germany quoted Milch's accusations about Messerschmitt's "remorseless lack of sympathy for the crash victims" and sweeping statements that his aircraft designs

The embattled genius, Professor Willy Messerschmitt. From his early youth, when he began designing and flying his own gliders, his destiny was clear: He would design the best aircraft in the world. In his own words, he summed up the Bf 109: "I made an attempt to equip the smallest possible light aircraft with a powerful engine, in order to produce a fighter which exceeded in its performance anything that had been seen before." *National Archives*

were "unsafe." Milch would remain Messerschmitt's harshest outspoken critic for years to come. The immediate effect was that Milch once again canceled the contract, then went two steps further: He demanded repayment of Lufthansa's investment *and* canceled an additional project to develop a high-speed courier aircraft for ferrying mail.

BFW had completely extended itself in the M.20 development and could not have paid back the money if its management had wanted to. A difficult court battle followed—one that conceivably could have forever ruined Messerschmitt's reputation as an aircraft designer. In the end, however, Lufthansa was forced by court order to honor the original contract for both airliners and courier aircraft. It saved BFW, which, by now, was in the throes of financial ruin and bankruptcy proceedings. A reorganization of the aircraft maker followed, and Messerschmitt became BFW's head. The M.20 went on to form the backbone of Lufthansa's fleet, providing reliable and safe service on internal German routes for more than a decade. Nevertheless, Milch's embittered feelings had been galvanized through the conflict, due partly to Messerschmitt's vehement retorts. Milch would later rise to the rank of field marshal and become Göring's deputy in the Luftwaffe. Through his high-ranking influence, the specter of the M.20 crashes would haunt Messerschmitt indefinitely.

Lean years followed, when BFW was tossed only scraps—relegated small contracts by the government to build aircraft designed by others under license, like 12 Heinkel He 45 biplanes. It was barely enough to keep the company solvent. Plus, it was adding insult to injury: Messerschmitt hated Ernst Heinkel almost as much as biplanes. So Messerschmitt turned his attention outside of Germany to win more substantial contracts to building aircraft that he himself designed.

He found promising business in neighboring Romania, where the national airline sought a new design. With specifications for an eight-seat passenger aircraft in hand, he was

Erhard Milch was Hermann Göring's deputy and Willy Messerschmitt's nemesis. The decision of selecting Germany's next fighter design lay largely in his hands. If he'd had any notion that the Bf 109 would actually *win* the competition for best design, he might have prevented Messerschmitt from entering. A highly competent administrator, Milch would be promoted to the rank of *Generalfeldmarshall* on July 19, 1940, just before the Battle of Britain. *National Archives*

The competition worked like this: The final choice of aircraft lay in the hands of Göring, under the advisement of Milch and also a World War I ace turned test pilot, Ernst Udet. The competing designers would submit designs for their aircraft and it was understood that anywhere along the process a design could be eliminated. Surviving designs would be given the go-ahead for fabrication into the prototype stage, in which three copies had to be constructed. After factory flight testing, the first prototype had to be flown to the Luftwaffen Test Center at Rechlin, where test pilots would put the aircraft through severe rigors. The pilots would report in detail on flight characteristics, such as rate of climb, speed in level flight, and maneuverability as measured by tight radius of turn and so on. Cost and ease of production were also factors. If two or more competitors were still in the running at this stage, the winning fighter would be chosen through flight tests the following year, in mid-1935, at Travemünde.

Due to the late invitation, Messerschmitt was already behind the others in the process. But he had a jump on the project in one respect: He'd already finalized the design for what was initially called the M-37, later to be called the Bf 108.[4] The Bf 108 was a four-place, single-engine sport plane that would bear a strong family resemblance to its fighting brother, the Bf 109. Not long after the Messerschmitt team began work designing the fighter, the Bf 108 (also christened *Taifun*, or Typhoon, by a well-known woman aviator, Elly Beinhorn, who'd flown the Bf 108) was impressing aviation enthusiasts across Europe.

Fueled by his confidence in the Bf 108, Messerschmitt drew liberally on its design to create the fighter. The Bf 109 also would have an enclosed cockpit, cantilevered low wings and fully retractable landing gear. They both would have an all-metal skin that was flush riveted. But the fighter fuselage would be much narrower, with a compact cockpit, as opposed to the doublewide seating of the Bf 108. Above all, the Bf 109 would adhere to "light and simple" principles that, as Messerschmitt biographer Frank Vann emphasizes, are the hallmarks of all Messerschmitt designs.

A key engineer assisting Messerschmitt on the Bf 109 project was Walter Rethel, who had once headed design at Kondor Aircraft Works. Rethel brought with him the experience in fighter design that Messerschmitt lacked (fulfilling that same role for the Bf 108 project had been Robert Lusser, who left before work began on the Bf 109 to design the V-1 flying bomb).

Another man in Messerschmitt's corner was Ernst Udet, soon to be appointed head of the Technical Office of the Air Ministry, the government agency that helped determine which aircraft would be ordered into mass production. Interested in Messerschmitt's innovations, Udet visited BFW's Augsburg facility a number of times. The two became fast friends, sharing passion for aviation and similar philosophies in aircraft design. Udet's recognition

delighted to return to the BFW plant in Augsburg and begin work on a fresh new project without the old baggage of animosity from his own government. However, after completion of the prototype, designated M-36, an official rebuke came from the German government, compliments of Erhard Milch. Milch's statement (delivered via a subordinate named *Oberstleutnant* Wilhelm Wimmer from the Luftwaffe's technical office) pointed to a lack of patriotism "when Germany was in great need of aircraft manufacturers."

Messerschmitt, through spokesmen at BFW, protested the obvious. It was *because* they received no government contracts that they had to look for business outside the country.

A Late Invitation to Compete

At the same time Messerschmitt had his hand slapped for not showing patriotic spirit, the competition to find the best front-line fighter design was heating up. Arado, Heinkel, and Focke-Wulf had already embarked on the design process when Wimmer finally invited BFW to enter the competition. In the same breath, he unofficially assured Messerschmitt that he had all but no chance of winning.

of Messerschmitt's genius would make him an indispensable advocate in the competition to come.

Before the end of 1934, metal already was being cut for the Bf 109 prototypes. By Luftwaffe specification, the design was supposed to be powered by the new 610-horsepower Junkers Jumo 210 engine. But since the fighter design development was moving along faster than the powerplant development, the engines were not yet available. The competitors, including Messerschmitt, had to use the 695-horsepower British Rolls-Royce Kestrel V-12 engine. It would be coupled with a Schwarz two-blade wooden propeller.

By September of the following year, a prototype Bf 109V-1 (V = experimental) was complete. With its first flight test in mid-September, the Bf 109 took to the skies months before its arch-adversary and British counterpart, the Supermarine Spitfire. After testing, BFW test pilot Hans Knoetsch flew it from Augsburg to the Luftwaffen Test Center at Rechlin, where the fighter designs were unveiled, and test pilots and engineers would conduct preliminary tests before final tests later at Travemünde.

As Knoetsch skillfully guided the Bf 109V-1 into the approach to Rechlin, he realized that many onlookers had gathered to await the arrival of the Bf 109. So he took advantage of the opportunity to put on a brief, impromptu show over the field. Many of the observers must have taken pause as they watched this trim, martial shape—thrilling and unfamiliar—barrel roll across the sky. First to catch the onlooker's eye were the sinister contours of a low canopy and long fuselage aft of the wings, accentuated by tiny tail surfaces. The aircraft spoke for itself, a machine made purely for speed and dealing destruction.

As the Bf 109 swooped low, some observers craned their necks to see over the top of the antiquated high wings of a few Heinkel 51 biplanes scattered on the field. Knoetsch pulled back on the stick and darted skyward, offering a dramatic juxtaposition of tomorrow's aircraft over yesterday's.

As the V1 began its final approach, Knoetsch cranked down the narrow landing gear beneath him. But like a stunning woman who gracefully enters a room before an approving public then shatters the moment by stumbling, the Bf 109 touched down in a perfect three-point landing—and, with a sudden sideways darting of the tail, the landing gear promptly collapsed. After the start of a ground loop, the aircraft arced through a short, spark-showered skid and came to an abrupt stop at a rakish angle—one wing high, supported by a bent but persevering undercarriage leg, its other wingtip resting on the ground. There was only minor damage and wounded pride.

It was a picture that would be repeated many times. This early mishap on the ground foretold of a weakness that would plague the aircraft its entire operational life. It was true that Rechlin airfield had a rough surface—much rougher than the home airfield at Augsburg. But on both rough and smooth surfaces, this was the first of countless ground loops and fractured undercarriages.

The track of the V1's undercarriage was absurdly narrow. The original thought was that the wings could be removed without cradling the aircraft if the landing gear was attached far inboard at the sides of the narrow fuselage. The prototype had legs almost vertical in attitude that made a track even narrower than later models.

German officials at the scene directed that the wheels must be spread wider apart to improve stability on the ground. Messerschmitt was not given time to return his machine to Augsburg, so a field expedient modification to cant the legs resulted in the splayed stance that the aircraft type would possess from then on. This helped, but by no means solved the problem.

Instability due to narrowness wasn't the only criticism surrounding the landing gear. To begin with, the fuselage rested at a steep ground angle, its nose pointing high above the horizon. While taxiing, a pilot could see nothing but sky through the tiny windscreen and had to strain for oblique views through the side glass. (The design of the canopy, hinged on the pilot's left, also thwarted visibility, because it could not be left open for taxi or takeoff.) Messerschmitt

The Heinkel He 51 was the standard fighter for the rejuvenating Luftwaffe of the early 1930s. Many thought that Germany's next-generation fighter should follow the He 51's pattern—bi-wing, open cockpit, and highly maneuverable, as measured by tight-turning capability. *Bowers Collection*

Willy Messerschmitt's innovative design: The four-seat Bf 108 *Taifun*. Far ahead of its time, the *Taifun* would be imitated by many other designers. Messerschmitt himself borrowed liberally from the design to create the single-seat, single-engine fighter, the Bf 109. *National Archives*

traded pilot visibility for lower weight and the highest possible lift coefficient for landing approach.

Another criticism of the landing gear, which came directly from test pilot Knoetsch, was its manual operation, requiring the pilot to literally crank the wheels up into the wings and down again. Knoetsch wanted a power system, which was installed in the next models.

For all its problems on the ground, the Bf 109's knock-kneed awkwardness could not overshadow its excellent performance in the air. Rechlin's test pilots recognized this and gave the nod to the Bf 109 to continue in the competition.

Competing Prototypes

Focke-Wulf designed the only high-winged entrant. The most memorable part of the Fw 159V2 was the obtrusive bracing to support its overhead wing that parasoled above an enclosed cockpit. The Fw 159V2 was unceremoniously shelved—the first design to be eliminated.

The Arado Ar 80V2 was a monoplane with nonretractable landing gear and open cockpit. Arado and rival Heinkel had been favored at the outset, but now in toe-to-toe comparisons, Arado found itself outclassed, and out of the competition as well.

The Heinkel design team of brothers Siegried and Walter Gunter followed the safe tack, cautiously mixing the old and new: Although a monoplane, the He 112V1 projected broad, semielliptical wings 41 feet wide and an open cockpit. Heinkel's design was favored by many veteran biplane fighter pilots because it more closely resem-

bled the biplanes they were accustomed to. Change comes hard, especially when you're dealing with a machine to which men must entrust their lives. Combat veterans of World War I rated tight turns at the top of their list of dogfighting priorities, and the biwing design made this possible. They also favored an open cockpit that gave unlimited, unobstructed vision for flying and fighting. The Heinkel provided at least one of the two and had good turning radius, too.

With Focke-Wulf and Arado eliminated, only the Heinkel and Messerschmitt designs remained. But before the next testing hurdles at Travemünde, the second and third prototypes of each design had to be constructed. Workers bustled around the next two airframes taking shape on jackstands on the shop floor of the BFW plant. Designated Bf 109V-2, the second and third prototypes received the long-awaited powerplants. With the new Junkers Jumo 210A liquid-cooled, inverted V-12 engine, the overall fuselage length increased slightly, and weight increased by 80 pounds. At the same time, Messerschmitt struggled to improve the landing gear, strengthening and canting it according to precise engineering calculations that were impossible during the harried field modifications to the V1 at Rechlin.

The V2 prototypes were finally outfitted with armament, a crowning feature without which the machine was virtually pointless. Specifications called for two machine guns. That largely drove Messerschmitt's decision to invert the V-12 engine, making room for the two .30-caliber (7.9mm) weapons mounted inside the upper engine cowling, synchronized to fire through the propeller. Along with the guns came the need for a cooling vent behind the top of the spinner.

The aerial performance of the two V2s at Travemünde was as impressive as the V1, but the Heinkel prototypes had been equally good. Not surprisingly, some of the "old school" pilots preferred them. When it came time to compare scores and make the decision, the panel of test pilots (Udet among them) found test results so close that they could not choose a winner with any decisiveness. They hedged and declared a draw.

Neither Messerschmitt nor Heinkel walked away with a full-scale production contract. Instead, both were contracted to produce 10 more aircraft for additional testing.

Messerschmitt accepted the news as a matter of course. He remained characteristically cool and confident. He *had* come a long way since the "unofficial assurance" that he would not win, but as for his reputation, he still had absolutely nothing to lose.

His engineering mind had done its own comparison of the Heinkel design against his. There remained an unshakable confidence in his airplane, in both flight performance and relative ease of mass production. Beyond the fixation of the test pilots on flight performance, Messerschmitt's discerning eye had zeroed in on the Heinkel's wings—he was convinced that the semielliptical wings would give their manufacturer problems in mass produc-

The Focke-Wulf 159V-1. Although it had retractable landing gear and a single high wing, the Fw 159 was a throwback to the realm of World War I fighters. But to the "stone-age" aviators (in Galland's words) who fleshed out the upper echelons of the German Air Ministry, that wasn't altogether a bad thing. World War I aviation veterans *wanted* the handling characteristics of the old biplane design. *Bowers Collection*

tion, compared to the relatively simple trapezoidal wings of the Bf 109. Time would prove him right: government overseers soon took notice of the great difficulty in producing even 10 more He 112 prototypes to fulfill the short-run contract.

In the meantime, more was coming to light about another "competitor"—the future enemy across the English Channel. German intelligence services had learned even before the previous inconclusive competition at Travemünde

The exquisite Arado Ar 80V-1. Designed by World War I ace Walter Blume, the Ar 80 had an open cockpit and fixed undercarriage like World War I fighters. Although sleek and even delicate in appearance, the aircraft's performance was far below the Bf 109 and He 112. It was quickly eliminated from the competition. *Bowers Collection*

that the British had ordered a production run of 310 Supermarine Spitfires. Plus, intelligence reports noted a British specification that required "keeping up with the Jones'."

Spitfire armament would consist of *four* machine guns—outgunning the German fighter prototypes by two. That necessitated altering the specifications the Germans had dictated the year before.

Specs for the next German prototypes were changed to three guns—one more .30-caliber to be mounted between the cylinder banks to fire through the propeller hub. This late alteration caused the following Messerschmitt prototype to be designated Bf 109V-3.

Final Showdown

In November 1936, the trials reconvened at Travemünde. The two surviving designs of Heinkel and Messerschmitt were poised for a final showdown. Messerschmitt's chief test pilot, Dr. Herman Wurster, was at the controls this time. The competition called for 10 spins to port, 10 spins to starboard. Dr. Wurster took the aircraft beyond that—*way* beyond. His aerial choreography was a neck-snapping, heart-in-your-throat demonstration of 23 counterclockwise turns, followed immediately by 21 clockwise turns. The plane did not lapse into the flat spin that many veterans watched for and expected. Dr. Wurster then powered the machine past 23,000 feet before casually nosing earthward and plummeting almost straight down in a terminal velocity dive before pulling out in an eye-popping swoop low over the field. The performance left observers awestruck and babbling among themselves.

Eyes then turned expectantly to the He 112. Its pilot was not yet in the cockpit. The moment was electric with anticipation. Everyone wanted to see what the rival could do to best Dr Wurster, but the officials cut to the quick. The crowd grew quiet, stunned to hear the trial agenda would be interrupted. The decision already had been made.

Some say Heinkel's test pilot was intimidated by the performance of the Bf 109 and bowed out. Others believed the decision really had been made before the final trials. The determining factors were the lower cost to mass produce the Bf 109, and the British decision to accelerate production of the Spitfire, an aircraft similar in many respects to the Bf 109. The bottom line was the Bf 109 would be the Luftwaffe's first-line fighter. And Messerschmitt's BFW would build it.

Later, Messerschmitt would encapsulate the bitter struggles and crowning triumph of a decade in a letter published in February 1940 in the Wehrmacht's newspaper, *Front und Heimat*:

"Dear Comrades! When the Führer . . . gave the order for rearmament and militarization, we were still one of the small German aircraft companies without any national—let alone international—renown. With only a few workers and designers, we built aircraft for various nonmilitary purposes in quite modest numbers. Few people in

The Heinkel He 112V-1. One of four designs competing for Germany's next-generation fighter plane, the He 112 would prove to be a worthy contender. It shared with the Bf 109 a low wing and retractable landing gear. *Bowers Collection*

Heinkel designers still held out hope to best the Bf 109 with this later prototype, He 112V-3, but it was not to be. Although his design was rejected in the end at Travemünde, Ernst Heinkel continued working to refine the He 112. So sure was Heinkel of the superiority of his aircraft that he went ahead with some production models of the He 112B. This was done at his own risk and his own expense. The German government did not buy the aircraft; they were instead sold to Spain and Romania. *Bowers Collection*

The Bf 109V-4, prototype for the B-1, was the first to be armed with an MG 17 machine gun firing through the propeller hub (in addition to two cowl-mounted MG 17s). The increased armament resulted when the Air Ministry learned of Great Britain's eight-gun fighter prototypes. *Bowers Collection*

With the Bf 109's wings removed, one can see how the undercarriage attaches to the sides of the narrow fuselage. Through endless ground looping and collapsing landing gear, the narrow track of the wheels proved problematic throughout the fighter's entire operational life. One of the original reasons Messerschmitt favored this design for landing gear was that the fuselage could stand wingless in field conditions without being trestled up. *Bowers Collection*

Germany or abroad then knew of the Bavarian Aircraft Company, and nobody foresaw that Augsburg would one day be the birthplace of the best and fastest fighter aircraft in the world."[5]

The design of one aircraft transformed Messerschmitt from a struggling outsider into a household name almost overnight in Germany. With the advent of World War II, it became a household name throughout the world when spoken in the same breath as "109."

Bf 109V-1 Specifications

Dimensions—Wingspan: 32 feet, 4 1/2 inches. Length: 27 feet, 11 inches.

Powerplant—Rolls-Royce Kestrel upright V-12 liquid-cooled engine. Takeoff horsepower: 695.

Performance—Maximum speed: 292 miles per hour (at 13,100 feet). Ceiling: 26,300 feet.

No time was wasted before production. Once the choice for Germany's new fighter design was final, Willy Messerschmitt's factory in Augsburg immediately tooled up for manufacture on a larger scale. No one could know at this time the eventual magnitude of the production run: a record 33,000 Bf 109s would be built. *Bowers Collection*

RAPID EVOLUTION

Bf 109B through 109E-4

Even as the new Bf 109 dazzled everyone with its performance, there was still resistance from the "old school" about what a fighter should be. Among the young blood of the Luftwaffe, Adolf Galland later described the debate this way:

> The old fighter pilots from the First World War, who were now sitting 'at the joystick' of the Supreme Command of the Luftwaffe with Göring at their head, had a compulsory gap of fifteen years behind them, during which they had probably lost contact with the rapid development of aviation. They were stuck on the idea that maneuverability in banking was primarily the determining factor in air combat. The Me 109 had, of course, much too high a stress per wing area and too great a speed to have such qualities. They could not, or simply would not, see that for modern fighter aircraft the tight turn as a form of aerial combat represented the exception, and, further, that it was quite possible to see, shoot and fight from an enclosed cockpit. In addition to other erroneous concepts it was feared that the higher takeoff and landing speed of the Me 109 would set insoluble aviation problems. All of this was proved, of course, to be false in practice, and today it sounds almost like a legend from the stone age of aviation.

The perfect testing grounds for new theories took the form of a small-scale, convenient war—the Spanish Civil War. It was a first step in moving aviation out of the "stone age." The Bf 109 was just on the brink of production, after several prototypes, as internal conflict in Spain erupted into all-out war.

Hitler threw his weight behind the Nationalist cause, led by Generalissimo Francisco Franco. The Russians were already backing the leftist Republicans by equipping them with the latest in Russian military hardware, including air-

Adolf Galland became commander of the Luftwaffe fighter arm at age 29 and was promoted to the rank of general at age 30. In the Luftwaffe, rank often lagged behind command appointment. At the rank of major in 1940, Galland was already *Kommodore* of *Jagdgeschwader* 26. As the "fighter pilot's fighter pilot," he would have many victories in Bf 109s. *National Archives*

craft. This meant the Bf 109 would be pitted against other new fighters of the world (including a few American fighters). It was the ideal test and became a veritable springboard that would launch a rapid evolution of the Bf 109.

The Bf 109 would go through a long succession of versions that incrementally improved altitude, firepower, and range. The Spanish Civil War precipitated the first, rapid advancements that built upon the basic prototype. The differences between some versions were almost imperceptible to a pilot. Others were more pronounced, with dramatic advancements in flight and fighting capability. Versions Bf 109B through Bf 109E-4 (those leading up to the Battle of Britain) are covered in this chapter. Subsequent versions are covered in chapter 6.

Bf 109 Action in Spain

German forces serving in Spain were called *Legion Condor* (including both air and ground components). The vanguard of *Legion Condor* arrived in Spain in April 1936, and by November of that year three *Staffeln* became operational. The fighters were commanded by Lieutenant General Wolfram von Richthofen, a cousin of the legendary World War I ace, the Red Baron, Manfred von Richthofen.

The Bf 109's first opponents: The Russian Polikarpov I-15 (above) and I-16 (right). When it first flew in December 1933, the stubby I-16 was the most advanced fighter in the world, with its cantilevered wing, variable pitch propeller, retractable landing gear, and 20mm cannon. About 500 were sent to Spain where, at first, they often triumphed against the He 51s of *Legion Condor*. When the Bf 109 entered battle, the tables turned completely. Faring even worse against the Bf 109 in Spanish skies was the I-15. Capable of 225 miles per hour, the I-15 took biplane fighter design to its peak, but became instantly archaic with the introduction of the fast new monoplane. Later, more than 2,200 of the tiny biwing fighters would be lost in the first week of Germany's Operation *Barbarossa*. *National Archives*

Both the He 51, shown here, and Bf 109 served in *Legion Condor*. At the same time the He 51's obsolescence became readily apparent, the advanced mono-wing Bf 109 was shown to be the right choice as Germany's new fighter. Flying in support of Generalissimo Francisco Franco's Nationalist forces, this He 51 has the "Franco" markings of a black cross on a white rudder, and the reverse on the wings. The He 51's obvious shortcomings had caused the Bf 109 to be rushed to Spain in prototype form. *Bowers Collection*

Initially, the *Staffeln* were equipped with the old standard front-line fighter, the Heinkel He 51B biplane. These were challenged by Soviet I-16 fighters, known by the Russians as *Moscas* (flies) and by the Germans as the derogatory nickname of *Ratas* (rats). The Russians also sent I-15 fighters, called *Chatos* (flat noses) by the Germans. So embarrassingly inferior was the He 51B that it was enough, in Galland's words, to usher some old fighter pilots "at the joystick" of the Luftwaffe's Supreme Command into modern thinking. They rushed the Bf 109 into service, even before production models were ready.

Already in December 1936, three of the V-model prototypes were dismantled, packed semisecretly into wooden crates, and loaded on a ship bound for Spain. Because of the as-yet clandestine nature of Germany's involvement, their pilots traveled incognito as civilian passengers on board. The aircraft were: V3, WN760, D-IOQY; V4, WN878, D-IALY; and V5, WN879, D-IIGO. Mechanical problems plagued the prototypes during their three-month baptism of fire, but the Bf 109Vs were in the air enough to prove to flyers of both sides that a new champion had entered Spanish skies. A few months later, the prototypes were shipped back to Messerschmitt for analysis, along with complete reports on combat performance.

Soon, other Jumo-powered Bf 109s followed. The first production series was designated Bf 109B-1 (the "Bf 109A" series withered before the production stage due to lack of armament). Some were dispatched in April 1937 to the second squadron of *Jagdgruppe* 88—making this the first operational unit to be equipped with production models of the Bf 109. The Bf 109B-2 followed quickly on the heels of the B-1, reaching Spain in sufficient numbers by the following July that the first and second squadrons of *Jagdgruppe* 88 were fully equipped with the new fighter. (The differences between the B-1 and B-2 subversions will be covered in detail on later pages of this chapter.) A total of 45 Bf 109Bs saw action in Spain. Later, smaller numbers of Bf 109Cs and Ds (still equipped with the Jumo engine) arrived in Spain.

In December 1938, the version that would become famous in the Battle of Britain—the Bf 109E with the new, long-awaited Daimler-Benz DB 601—arrived in the closing days of the conflict, too late to see action. The early Bf 109s had proved more than adequate, as *Legion Condor* clearly won air superiority in Spain.

Adolf Galland, then a mere *leutnant* (second lieutenant), remembered how the Bf 109Bs, Cs, and Ds "had proved their superiority against the strongest international competition. . . . The (109s) were mainly intended to combat the numerous Curtiss and *Rata* fighters, either as lone wolves or when escorting bomber formations. The Me 109 was definitely superior to them and shot down a great number. . . ."

In March 1939, *Legion Condor* completed its duty and returned to the Fatherland, triumphant in virtually all aspects of air and ground warfare. While helping Franco and his Nationalists win power, the Bf 109 had grown through adolescence and was reaching maturity. Tanks, other equipment and aircraft also were tested under actual combat conditions. But it was the Bf 109 that emerged as the crown jewel among the treasures of the arsenal. During the course of the war, *Legion Condor* fighter pilots had downed a total of 340 confirmed enemy aircraft with minimal losses due to enemy action.

The Bf 109's clear superiority was no surprise to Messerschmitt. However, he wanted to make his fighter even better. Through trial by fire in those combat testing grounds, he and his engineers relentlessly sought to identify flaws and weaknesses in the Bf 109. They continuously tweaked, tested, and modified the aircraft using all available technology.

Lessons Learned

Accelerated development propelled the Bf 109 through production versions B all the way to the E in less than two years. During the Bf 109's evolution in service with *Legion Condor*, the Germans faced a variety of challenges. Some were ingeniously overcome, others were *never* overcome during World War II.

A big challenge was armament. Messerschmitt and his engineers always favored fuselage-mounted (versus wing-mounted) armament. They clung to the idea of firing through the propeller hub. Abandoned and resurrected repeatedly, this idea seemed good because the heavy mass of the motor could absorb the recoil of the cannon, and it afforded straight-on aim.

In practice firing, the Bf 109V-4's engine-mounted 20mm MG/FFM cannon caused teeth-chattering vibration, yet the Bf 109B-2 with the same armament seemed to work well in combat. Later versions also had trouble. A second armament challenge persisted for the entire war: wing-mounted guns. Whereas the British contemporaries had been designed with wing-mounted armament in mind almost from the beginning, this was an add-on for the Bf 109. At the Augsburg factory, the Bf 109V-8 was the first fitted with a MG 17 machine gun in each wing, but engineers quickly saw the wings were simply not made to withstand the jarring recoil.

Messerschmitt's original design simply did not anticipate wing armament. Adhering to his lifelong design principals of simplicity and light weight, he had wrapped the most powerful powerplant available inside the smallest, most aerodynamic airframe possible.

A lot of care had gone into the wing design. Fixated on high-speed performance, Messerschmitt designed very thin wings. But what was good wing design for high speed was not good for slower speeds, especially in takeoff and landing. Messerschmitt's solution was automatic slots on the leading edge (unprecedented for a fighter) and slotted flaps to alter the air flow over the thin wings for slower speeds.

When the Bf 109B-1 burst into combat over Spain, its superiority was felt immediately. Among the first 10 to arrive, this B-1 saw service with the *Staffel* 2 of J/88. Note the Schwarz fixed-pitch propeller made of wood. Only 30 B-1s were produced before the Augsburg factory would upgrade to the B-2. The sole difference was the B-2's improved propeller—a variable-pitch VDM metal Hamilton-Standard. *Bowers Collection*

In early 1937, the first batch of production Bf 109s line the field at Augsburg. Although fighting raged in Spain, war seemed distant in this peaceful and well-ordered flight line, tucked into the heart of Bavaria. *Bowers Collection*

This left Messerschmitt with a free hand to create wings devoted solely to function—wings of aerodynamic purity, made exclusively for lift and speed.

Now, with the Bf 109 severely outgunned by enemy aircraft, the wings became *the* only alternative for the additional fixed forward firepower needed to keep pace. To Messerschmitt and his engineers, it must have been something like the feeling of a sculptor who had just finished a solid-granite statue masterpiece and then was informed it must gush water like a fountain.

The flitting of the wings caused by machine gun recoil could be overcome by a general strengthening at key points. Positioning of the gun muzzles themselves was key, because trim could be skewed when firing. Yet the guns needed to be outside the wheel well. The aileron control surfaces needed balancing to overcome the flutter. The wing's leading edge required strengthening, as did the single spar. Engineers went ahead with a general strengthening of the existing wing design to accommodate the machine guns, which ushered in the next letter of the alphabet, the Bf 109C version.

The progression to the wing-mounted 20mm cannon was then inevitable. With that came even more punishing recoil that necessitated another redesign of the wing. Test firing of cannons mounted on prototypes sent shudders through the wing so violently that it threatened failure of the wing structure. The right balance of strength and aerodynamics wouldn't be struck for a long time (until production of the E version). The new wing now had a bulge underneath for the cannon-shell drum. All this continued to erode the clean and simple lines of Messerschmitt's pristine design, now swollen here and there on its nose and belly and wings.

It wasn't only the shape, structure, armament, and powerplant that evolved during the *Legion Condor* experience. The *way* the fighter was flown in combat evolved, too: There were the new formations of the two-man *Rotte* and four-man *Schwarm*. As RAF Group Captain J. E. Johnson explained: "Credit must be given to the Germans for devising the perfect fighter formation. It was based on what they called the *Rotte*, that is, the element of two fighters. Some 200 yards separated a pair of fighters and the main responsibility of the number two, or wingman, was to guard his leader from the quarter or an astern attack. Meanwhile the leader navigated his small force and covered his wingman.

None of this addressed armament in the wings. But then, Messerschmitt hadn't needed to. Recall that the Air Ministry's original specifications prior to the fighter showdown at Rechlin and Travemünde called for *two* machine guns. It was really Ernst Udet, Messerschmitt's champion, who insisted on the priorities of speed, rate of climb, and tight turning radius, even at the cost of heavier armament. To fulfill armament specifications, Messerschmitt inverted the V-12 engine and mounted the guns on top, synchronized to fire through the propeller.

Based closely on the V4, V5, and V6 prototypes, the Bf 109B-2 shown is powered by a Jumo 210E with 640 horsepower. Note the protruding underwing oil cooler, which would be drastically modified to decrease drag in later versions. *Bowers Collection*

The *Schwarm*, four fighters, simply consisted of two pairs, and when we eventually copied the Luftwaffe and adopted this pattern we called it the 'finger-four' because the relative positions of the fighters are similar to a plan view of one's finger tips."

Bf 109B-1 and B-2

As alluded to earlier, the Bf 109A version was never produced, because the Germans learned in the midst of design that the British had stepped up armament specifications of its new monoplane fighters—twice the armament planned for the first production Bf 109. Immediately, the puny two-gun armament planned for the Bf 109A was judged inadequate before the first aircraft could be fabricated from the design on paper. So, the first of the production versions became the Bf 109B-1.

The first Bf 109B-1 rolled out on its splayed landing gear from the Augsburg-Haunstetten assembly line[6] in February 1937. The business end of the new fighter included three MG 17 machine guns, two above the engine with muzzles that lay recessed, jutting into blast troughs molded in the cowl. The third was engine-mounted and fired through the propeller hub, where no synchronization was needed. Since the engine-mounted machine gun jammed easily because of overheating, this third gun was removed from some newly built aircraft and not installed to begin with on aircraft later in the production run. Cooling problems for the top two nose guns were resolved with minor retooling that made three slots in the cowl and a small vent on the machine gun access panel just before the windscreen. Pilots aimed the guns through a Carl Zeiss *Reflexvisier* C/12C reflector gunsight.

The B-1 powerplant was the latest of the Jumos, the 210Da. It was coupled with a fixed-pitch wooden Schwarz airscrew capable of 292 miles per hour at 13,100 feet. From a dead stop on the runway, it clawed its way to an altitude of 19,685 feet in just less than 10 minutes—a rate of climb not pleasing to pilots.

The solution was a new variable-pitch, metal propeller: The Hamilton-Standard, designed in the United States. The new propeller was tested on the prototype Bf 109V-7 with good results.[7] How ironic that, on the brink of war, the first production Bf 109s had American airscrews, sold under license, and British wing slats, compliments of Handley-Page!

By fall 1937, Bf 109B-2s became more plentiful. Many were shipped directly from the factory to *Legion Condor* in Spain. *Bowers Collection*

Bf 109B-2 Specifications

Dimensions—Wingspan: 32 feet, 4 1/2 inches. Length: 28 feet, 6 1/2 inches. Height: 8 feet, 1/2 inch.

Weight—Empty: 3,483 pounds. Gross: approximately 4,857 pounds.

Powerplant—Junkers Jumo 210E or 210G inverted V-12 liquid-cooled engine. Takeoff horsepower: 640 or 670, respectively. (This compares to 635 horsepower for B-1's Jumo 210Da.)

Armament—Two 7.9mm Rheinmetall-Borsig MG 17 machine guns, mounted above the engine in the cowl.

Performance—Maximum speed: 298 miles per hour (at 13,100 feet). Maximum range: 430 miles. Ceiling: 31,200 feet.

The Hamilton-Standard two-blade propeller was the segue into the B-2 designation after fewer than 30 B-1s were produced. Other refinements to the Bf 109B-2 included:

- The Jumo 210E with a two-stage supercharger generating 640 horsepower, and soon after the Jumo 210G with 670 horsepower, both coupled with a variable-pitch metal propeller.
- Improved oil cooler efficiency when mounted under the port wing (instead of with the radiator bath).
- A single wire for the FuG R/T antenna (versus three wires).
- Heavier framing around the windscreen.

The first production Bf 109Bs were immediately shipped to *Legion Condor*. They were welcomed by German pilots who had been repeatedly humbled in the old He 51Bs.

Bf 109C-1, C-2, and C-3

The Bf 109C series superseded the B version in the first months of 1938. Prototypes for the C version were the Bf 109V-8, V-9, and V-10.

The most important changes were increases in armament. In addition to the B-1's two cowl guns, the C-1 had four machine guns (two wing mounted); the C-2 had five machine guns (the fifth firing through the propeller hub); and the C-3 had those four machine guns *and* a cannon firing through the propeller hub. The advent of the wing guns required the wing modification described earlier.

U.S. Army Air Corps' tests on a captured Bf 109 described armament design this way: "Control of all weapons is from the pilot's cockpit, by a mechanical pneumatic remote control installation. A reflex sight is used, located at eye level of the pilot behind the slanting windshield. When machine guns are used, the weapons are entirely housed in the wing and cooling is by air ducts. Carrying off of air and powder gases is by cut-outs in the wing trailing edge. Installation is such that a convenient interchange of guns, especially of the breech mechanism, is possible. Accessibility is by hinged cover with quick release so that mounting and dismounting of the complete weapons is possible within a few minutes."

Flight-related advancements included:

- Small extenders on exhaust pipes to improve expulsion of hot gasses away from the cowl.

Two Bf 109Cs are serviced in Czechoslovakia sometime during 1938. The shield emblem below the windscreen had a black outline, white background, and red cursive R signifying JG 2 Richthofen (*Jagdgeschwadern* often bore the namesake of famous aces, alive or dead). Note the small extenders on the exhaust pipes—one visible differentiator of the C version, versus the B, which had only a series of oval slots cut in the side of the cowl. *Bowers Collection*

A sleeker nose characterizes the Bf 109D-1. This example is said to be powered by the scarce DB 600 engine. Since few Daimler-Benz engines were available at the time the Dora went into production, most were equipped with the Jumo 210. In all, only about 200 Doras were built—an interim solution before the vaunted Daimler-Benz engines would be available in volume. And by then, the next series of Bf 109—the hybrid Emil—would be designed. *Bowers Collection*

- Wing modification to strengthen the leading edge that accommodated wing-mounted MG 17 machine guns.
- The Junkers Jumo 210Ga engine with fuel injection (far superior to a normal float carburetor system) that enabled inverted flight and negative-g dives.
- A radiator with a larger intake, offering more effective cooling (but causing more drag).

Bf 109C Series Specifications

Dimensions—Wingspan: 32 feet, 4 1/2 inches. Length: 28 feet, 2/3 inch. Height: 8 feet, 1/2 inch.

Weight—Empty: 3,522 pounds. Gross: approximately 5,062 pounds.

Powerplant—Junkers Jumo 210Ga inverted V-12 liquid-cooled engine. Takeoff horsepower: 700.

Armament—C-1: Four 7.9mm Rheinmetall-Borsig MG 17 machine guns, two mounted above the engine in the cowl and two wing-mounted. C-2: C-1's armament plus an engine-mounted MG 17. C-3: C-1's armament plus one 20mm Oerlikon MG FF engine-mounted cannon.

Performance—Maximum speed: 292 miles per hour at 14,765 feet. Maximum range: 405 miles.

Bf 109D

The word for *D* in the German phonetic alphabet is "Dora." This became the moniker of the version. However, the more apt word for *D* in Willy Messerschmitt's experience might have been "disappointment."

The Bf 109D was to be the first equipped with the venerable Daimler-Benz DB 600 engine so long in coming. Recall that the very first fighter prototypes, built on the Air Ministry's specs for the 1934 competition, were to be designed with the DB 600 powerplant in mind. In the interim, the Jumo had filled the void. But now the DB 600s were being produced in good number, and with it, the Bf109 was to finally reach the full potential envisioned.

But airframes stood unfinished on the line awaiting powerplant installation. The engines didn't come. Instead, the priority for the engine went to the Heinkel bomber, the He 111, which also used the DB 600. The rationale was that the bomber was the mainstay of the coming offensive. In the spring of 1938, when the Dora design was ready for the assembly line, Hitler was already thinking of invasion in the East and West (which meant bombers). Daimler-Benz engineers offered a conciliatory promise that an even better engine, the DB 601, soon would be available for Messerschmitt's fighter.

A handful of DB 600 engines were doled out for the Doras, mainly as part of a ruse to lead future enemies into thinking that an advanced version was already in production and plentiful. In actuality, the production went on, but the airframes continued being fitted with the Jumo 210. So in essence, the Bf 109D was a marginally improved Bf 109C.

The Bf 109V-14 was one of the prototypes for the Emil series. It carries the classic angular lines of the early square-winged versions. *Bowers Collection*

Bf 109E-4

1. Hollow propeller hub
2. Spinner
3. Three-bladed VDM variable-pitch propeller
4. Propeller pitch-change mechanism
5. Spinner back plate
6. Glycol coolant header tank
7. Glycol filler cap
8. Cowling fastener
9. Chin intake
10. Coolant pipe fairing
11. Exhaust forward fairing
12. Additional oil tank (for long-range)
13. Daimler-Benz DB 601A engine
14. Supplementary intakes
15. Fuselage machine-gun troughs
16. Anti-vibration engine mounting pads
17. Exhaust ejector stubs
18. Coolant pipes (to underwing radiators)
19. Oil cooler intake
20. Coolant radiator
21. Radiator outlet flap
22. Cowling frame
23. Engine mounting support strut
24. Spent cartridge collector compartment
25. Ammunition boxes (starboard loading)
26. Supercharger
27. Supercharger air intake fairing
28. Forged magnesium alloy cantilever engine mounting
29. Engine mounting/forward bulkhead attachment
30. Ammunition feed chutes
31. Engine accessories
32. Two cowl-mounted MG 17 machine guns
33. Blast tube muzzles
34. Wing skin
35. Starboard cannon access
36. 20-mm MG FF wing cannon
37. Leading-edge automatic slot
38. Slot tracks
39. Slot-actuating linkage
40. Wing main spar
41. Intermediate rib station
42. Wing end rib
43. Starboard navigation light
44. Aileron outer hinge
45. Aileron metal trim tab
46. Starboard aileron
47. Aileron/flap link connection
48. Combined control linkage
49. Starboard flap frame
50. Cannon ammunition drum access
51. Fuselage machine-gun cooling slots
52. Gun mounting frame
53. Firewall/bulkhead
54. Instrument panel near face (fabric covered)
55. Oil dipstick cover
56. Control column
57. Oil filler cap (tank omitted for clarity)
58. Rudder pedal assembly
59. Aircraft identity data plate (external)
60. Main spar center section carry-through
61. Under-floor control linkage
62. Oxygen regulator
63. Harness adjustment lever

64. Engine priming pump
65. Circuit breaker panel
66. Hood catch
67. Starboard-hinged cockpit canopy
68. Revi gunsight (offset to starboard)
69. Windscreen panel frame
70. Canopy section frame
71. Pilot's head armor
72. Pilot's back armor

73. Seat harness
74. Pilot's seat
75. Seat adjustment lever
76. Tailplane incidence handwheel
77. Cockpit floor diaphragm
78. Landing flaps control hand wheel
79. Seat support frame
80. Contoured L-shaped fuel tank
81. Tailplane incidence cables
82. Fuselage frame
83. Rudder cable
84. Oxygen cylinders (2)

86. Baggage compartment
87. Entry handhold (spring-loaded)
88. Canopy fixed aft section
89. Aerial mast
90. Aerial
91. Fuel filler cap
92. Fuel vent line
93. Radio pack support brackets
94. Anti-vibration bungee supports
95. FuG VII transmitter/receiver radio pack
96. Aerial lead-in
97. Tailplane incidence cable pulley
98. Rudder control cable

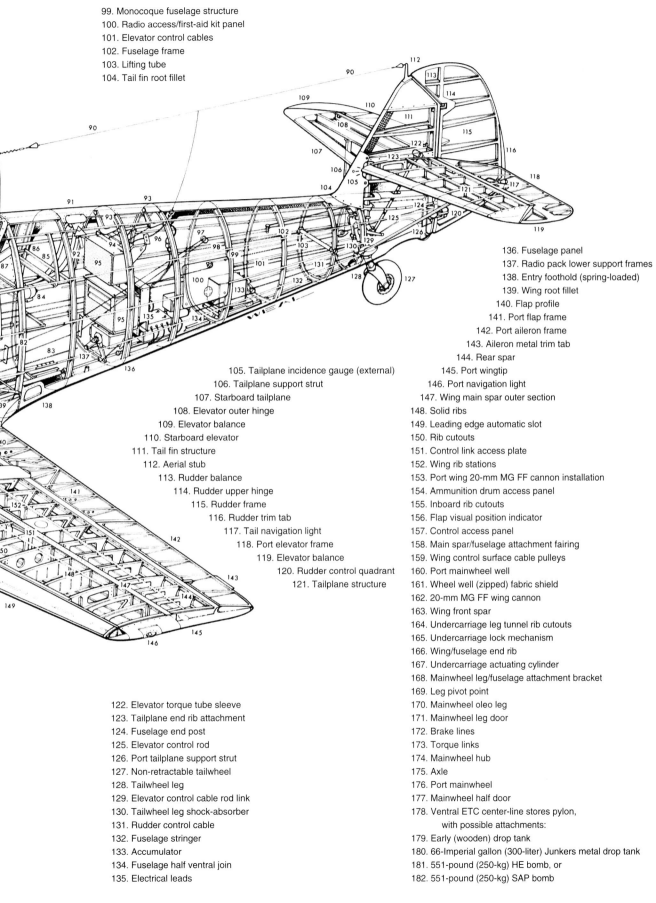

99. Monocoque fuselage structure
100. Radio access/first-aid kit panel
101. Elevator control cables
102. Fuselage frame
103. Lifting tube
104. Tail fin root fillet

105. Tailplane incidence gauge (external)
106. Tailplane support strut
107. Starboard tailplane
108. Elevator outer hinge
109. Elevator balance
110. Starboard elevator
111. Tail fin structure
112. Aerial stub
113. Rudder balance
114. Rudder upper hinge
115. Rudder frame
116. Rudder trim tab
117. Tail navigation light
118. Port elevator frame
119. Elevator balance
120. Rudder control quadrant
121. Tailplane structure

122. Elevator torque tube sleeve
123. Tailplane end rib attachment
124. Fuselage end post
125. Elevator control rod
126. Port tailplane support strut
127. Non-retractable tailwheel
128. Tailwheel leg
129. Elevator control cable rod link
130. Tailwheel leg shock-absorber
131. Rudder control cable
132. Fuselage stringer
133. Accumulator
134. Fuselage half ventral join
135. Electrical leads

136. Fuselage panel
137. Radio pack lower support frames
138. Entry foothold (spring-loaded)
139. Wing root fillet
140. Flap profile
141. Port flap frame
142. Port aileron frame
143. Aileron metal trim tab
144. Rear spar
145. Port wingtip
146. Port navigation light
147. Wing main spar outer section
148. Solid ribs
149. Leading edge automatic slot
150. Rib cutouts
151. Control link access plate
152. Wing rib stations
153. Port wing 20-mm MG FF cannon installation
154. Ammunition drum access panel
155. Inboard rib cutouts
156. Flap visual position indicator
157. Control access panel
158. Main spar/fuselage attachment fairing
159. Wing control surface cable pulleys
160. Port mainwheel well
161. Wheel well (zipped) fabric shield
162. 20-mm MG FF wing cannon
163. Wing front spar
164. Undercarriage leg tunnel rib cutouts
165. Undercarriage lock mechanism
166. Wing/fuselage end rib
167. Undercarriage actuating cylinder
168. Mainwheel leg/fuselage attachment bracket
169. Leg pivot point
170. Mainwheel oleo leg
171. Mainwheel leg door
172. Brake lines
173. Torque links
174. Mainwheel hub
175. Axle
176. Port mainwheel
177. Mainwheel half door
178. Ventral ETC center-line stores pylon,
    with possible attachments:
179. Early (wooden) drop tank
180. 66-Imperial gallon (300-liter) Junkers metal drop tank
181. 551-pound (250-kg) HE bomb, or
182. 551-pound (250-kg) SAP bomb

The advancements that *did* come with the Dora were:

- Greater armament with a 20mm MG FF cannon mounted between cylinder banks of the engine to fire through the spinner.
- A heavier main wing spar to accommodate the higher wing loading that would come with a heavier powerplant.
- A cantilevered tail-wheel shaft to replace a shaft with a bracing arm.
- The Revi C/12D gunsight to replace the less accurate Revi C/12C.

The life of a prototype was often painfully short. This Bf 109V-17, another forerunner to the E-3, met grief on a gentle undulation near Augsburg. The prototype had been fitted with the engine-mounted MG FF cannon that fired through the spinner. Whether or not the added armament precipitated the crash is unknown. *Bowers Collection*

Bf 109D Specifications (of the relative few that actually had the new Daimler-Benz powerplant)

Dimensions—Wingspan: 32 feet, 4 1/2 inches. Length: 28 feet, 2 1/2 inches. Height: 7 feet, 3 1/2 inches.

Weight—Empty: 3,964 pounds. Gross (with pilot, fuel, and ammunition): approximately 5,335 pounds.

Powerplant (intended)—Daimler-Benz DB 600Aa inverted V-12 liquid-cooled engine. Takeoff horsepower: 960.

Armament—Two 7.9mm Rheinmetall-Borsig MG 17 machine guns, mounted above the engine in the cowl and one 20mm Oerlikon MG FF engine-mounted cannon.

Performance—Maximum speed: 357 miles per hour at 11,480 feet. Maximum range: 348 miles. Ceiling: 34,500 feet.

Bf 109E-1, E-2, E-3, and E-4

The Bf 109E would become the principal fighter for 1939–40—the critical *blitzkrieg* years that included the Battle of Britain. It would tout the powerful Daimler-Benz engine, available in increasing numbers by early 1939.

Only weeks before the first Bf 109Es were produced, in late 1938, the DB 601A engine had been certified for use in single-engine aircraft (namely, the Emil). The engine was actually built by three different manufacturers: Daimler-Benz at Marienfelde and Genshagen, as well as the Henschel Flugmotorenbau at Altenbauna and Bussing-Werke at Braunschweig.

The DB 601A was much like the DB 600, with the same cylinder bore and stroke, but a compression ratio improved from 6.5 to 6.9. That, along with the improved supercharger, helped boost horsepower from 960 to 1,100. It continued to burn the standard 87-octane fuel.

With the DB powerplant, the Bf 109 was certainly faster, but what did the heavier, more powerful engine do for flight characteristics? Weight had reached 5,534 pounds for the E-1, an increase of nearly 500 pounds over the C-1. Turning radius widened slightly, and the controls became slightly heavier, by some accounts. Otherwise, handling was not affected adversely. With flaps at 20 degrees, take-offs were short and rate of climb outstanding. Its stall speed was high, but pilots could easily feel aileron vibrations as well as other advance-warning signals.

A flight test in fall 1939 performed by the French Air Ministry described flight characteristics this way: "from the pilot's point of view, the . . . aileron control is brilliant and the plane can be tipped from one wing tip to the other in the brief time in which the stick can be pushed over. The elevators are light and harmonize well with the ailerons while the rudder is considerably less responsive but is adequate in a spin. There have been rumors that the Me 109 is nose heavy. The angle of climb is very steep; the pilot sees nothing ahead of him but sees the ground to the rear. In level flight, visibility is very good in the axis of flight and above, poor on the sides and to the rear, nil vertically and toward the ground in the sector up to 60 degrees to the front and 20 degrees to the rear. The airplane appears unstable longitudinally at full throttle and at low speed; resulting from the above, a steady aim in the dive or climb can be maintained only by use of the stabilizer. The ailerons give efficient control even at low speeds. However, they have a tendency to become still at high speeds. The most noted peculiarity is the poor compensation for engine torque, which makes it very difficult to turn to the right in a climb."

Prototypes for the Bf 109E, the V-14 and V-15, were the first with DB 601A powerplants. The engine featured a Bosch fuel injection system. The DB 601A put the fighter in a class of its own—arguably the best in the world at the time.

Knowing the advancements, Ulrich Steinhilper, later an ace in JG 52, was irrepressibly anxious to try the new Emil. He later described the experience:

"The squadrons were converting from the Me 109D to the Me 109E . . . I walked to the hangar for Number 1 Squadron, where I knew a factory-fresh 109E had just arrived. It had not been assigned, and so I told the mechanic who was servicing it to get me a parachute and prepare the aircraft for immediate flight. He unquestioningly carried out my instructions; discipline in our unit was tight and NCOs would not normally question the orders of an officer. I strapped on my parachute and climbed up onto the port wing of the 109, pausing to ask the mechanic if there was anything new in handling notes on this 109E. It was quite different to the old 'Dora.' The Junkers Jumo engine, which weighed 440 kilograms (972 pounds) and produced a modest 630 horsepower, had been replaced by the DB 601, which was slightly heavier at 600 kilograms (1,326 pounds) but produced a phenomenal 1,100 horsepower. The mechanic said that he thought that the 'Emil' landed best if flown in at about 10–15 kilometers per hour (6.2–9.3 miles per hour) faster than the 'Dora.'

"Somewhat ner-vously I stepped into the cockpit and dropped down into the close-fitting interior. The air-craft smelled new with a rich mix-ture of odors; parts still being 'burned off' as the engine began to gain hours and the new parts still being covered with preservative and fresh paint. The mechanic helped to strap me in and I began my preflight checks. All was in order. I gave the signal to clear prop and start and the 'Black Man' who was standing on the star-board wing-root began to wind the heavy eclipse starter. At the right moment I pulled the lever and the starter turned the great DB 601 engine over, roaring into life on the first turn. The whole airframe shook with the power as I made my running checks prior to takeoff. Again all was in order, and so I gave the signal to clear chocks and I released the brakes. Taxiing around to line up, I opened the throttle and the aircraft leapt forward, the long engine cowling clearing my view as the tail came up smartly. I was soon in the air.

"The takeoffs weren't too different, there was a no-ticeable surge of power and the aircraft seemed to lift off in a shorter run, but once in the air the handling didn't differ too much. The landings, in contrast, were a bit of a fight. Cutting back on power for the landing seemed to make the aircraft plunge, losing height much faster than I was used to. Another problem, which was to prove crucial in my undoing, was a gravel road that crossed the line of the runway. On this day it was approached at an angle and was very slightly raised—not enough to cause a problem under normal conditions, but things were going too well.

"I was attempting to find the upper end of the limits for approach speed and was going faster than on the previ-ous approaches. I was pleased—this seemed to be it. The landing was soft and the aircraft handled perfectly. I was almost congratulating myself when I crossed the gravel roadway, which caused the aircraft to jump up a little, fly-ing again for a few brief moments. In those split seconds I must have recalled my experience of the new aircraft be-ing heavy and tending to drop at low speed. I decided to give it a short shot of throttle, just to keep the nose up. I might have gotten away with that on the 'Dora,' but not with the 'Emil.'

The fighter gets collateral duties. Called a *Jabo* in its fighter-bomber role, the Bf 109E-4/B shown here is fitted with an electrically operated rack, to which a 250-kilogram (552.5-pound) bomb is mounted. Beginning in fall 1940, the *Jabo* role was a chore that fighter pilots did not relish.
Ethell Collection, Bowers Collection

"What hap-pened in those few seconds can be reconstructed by examining the different charac-teristics of the two types of 109. The 'Dora' had a single-blade prop and relatively low-powered en-gine. The 'Emil' had a much heav-ier three-bladed prop and nearly twice the power of the 'Dora.' My quick 'shot of throttle' released 1,100 horsepower onto a heavy propeller, causing a sharp torque reaction in the aircraft, making the fuselage turn on its own axis in the opposite direction to the propeller. The result was that my left wing dropped and touched the ground. Again, there had to be a decision in a split second, and so I kicked the rudder hard to the right to bring her round straight again and cause the wing to rise a little or at least to take the impact away from the wingtip. That worked OK, but I still had lots of forward momentum, which threw the aircraft onward at an angle of about 45 degrees relative. The starboard undercarriage leg hit first and folded under, virtually snapping off, with the port leg being bent outward at a hideous angle. The big three-bladed prop hit the ground and began a creditable job of plowing the airfield while it was

27

After this captured Emil went through testing rigors at RAE Farnborough, it was turned over to the United States (more than a year before the United States officially entered the war). More testing followed, and the resultant U.S. Army Air Corps report from November 1940 described the E-3 this way: "The Me-109 conforms to modern aircraft

design of all-metal construction, stressed skin, monocoque fuselage, and flush rivets. The wings, trapezoidal in plan form, are of the single spar design with fabric covered flaps located between the fuselage and ailerons, which are mechanically operated. The ailerons are fabric covered and droop slightly to decrease the landing speed. The horizontal strut-braced stabilizer is adjustable. Slots along the leading edge of the wing automatically enter into operation at speeds below 112 miles per hour. The fuel tank is built roughly in the shape of a chair and fits behind and beneath the pilot's seat. The tank is protected from gunfire. The cantilever type landing gear is retracted outwardly and upwardly into the wings by a hydraulic system or, in an emergency, by mechanical device. The pitch of the three-blade V.D.M. propeller is controlled in flight by a controllable motor from a switch on the instrument board. A complete set of navigational, power plant, and flight control instruments are provided for and include a propeller pitch indicator, landing gear position indicator, low fuel supply indicator, and a Bosch (horn) that sounds when the flaps are lowered before the landing gear. The two-way radio is located behind the pilot's cockpit." *National Archives*

twisted and bent backward like thin tinfoil.

"As suddenly as the cacophony of noise and tortured metal had begun, it was over and I sat in silence, the harness straps biting into my shoulders and chest. The only sound was the odd 'ping' of hot metal cooling."

The Emil was virtually brand new from the firewall forward. In addition to the DB 601A engine came these advancements:

• An improved supercharger that increased output.
• A redesigned chin. The radiator, along with its wide-mouthed intake, was removed from beneath the motor and took the form of two radiators, one under each wing. (In its place on the chin now was the oil cooler with a smaller intake.)

Armament for the E-1 remained the same as the C and D versions, two cowl-mounted machine guns and a machine gun on each wing. It also retained the FuG R/T equipment.

The Bf 109E-2 had a very brief life. It was yet another attempt to use the engine-mounted cannon. But again, vibration and overheating and jamming sent the engineers back to the drawing board.

The Luftwaffe still yearned for the punch of the cannon, however. Despite its slower rate of fire, the cannon proved more effective.Enter the Bf 109E-3 and E-4, famed fighters in the Battle of Britain. With the E-3, the most powerful armament was paired up with the most powerful powerplant yet. After failed attempts for a nose cannon, wing mounting became the only viable option. So, the E-3's wings were redesigned to accommodate the larger ammunition drum and withstand the recoil of cannons.

The two cowl-mounted machine guns, as always, were retained. The E-3 carried ammunition of 1,000 rounds per machine gun and 60 rounds for each cannon.

Until this time, most of the Emils in service were underarmed E-1s with only four 7.9mm MG 17 machine guns. These were inferior in firepower to the Spitfires and Hurricanes, each with eight machine guns. But with the E-3's two wing-mounted MG FF 20mm cannons, the Bf 109 had firepower superiority for the first time—outranging and outgunning both RAF fighters. Its cannon fire could blast crippling holes in thin-gauge skin and crumple the internal framework of any enemy aircraft.

The first Bf 109E-3s were delivered in fall 1939 to II/JG 54. Within weeks, on November 22, a brand-new E-3 was also inadvertently delivered into *Allied* hands, when an aircraft assigned to II/JG 54 bellied in near Worth, France. This E-3 was evaluated extensively by the French, then turned over to the British for evaluation and finally to the USAAF. By early 1940, E-3s were the most numerous in the *Jagdgeschwadern*.

With lessons learned during the blitzkrieg in Poland, the Battle of France, and the preliminaries to the Battle of Britain, the Bf 109E-4 came into being in May 1940. Changes from the E-3 included:

- A square-cornered, heavier-framed canopy and swept-back windscreen.
- Replacement of the wing-mounted cannon with MG FF M type (this fired improved ammunition).
- Elimination of the engine-mounted cannon.

Emil Jabos

Messerschmitt engineers began experimenting with the Bf 109E-1 as a fighter-bomber, or *Jabo*, during the Battle of France. Designated the Bf 109E-1/B, the fighter was fitted with a makeshift ventral bomb rack centered between the wings and tested with bombs weighing 50 to 250 kilograms (110.5 to 552.5 pounds). The pilot released the bomb with an electric switch.

The retrofitted racks on the E-1s usually carried 50-kilogram (110.5-pound) bombs. E-4/Bs built on the assembly line as *Jabos* handled four 50-kilogram (110.5-pound) bombs or one 250-kilogram (552.5-pound) bomb. Testing went to the next stage during the Battle of the Channel: *Erprobungsgruppe* 210 was an experiment that sent bomb-toting Bf 109E-4Bs and Bf 110C-4Bs over the Channel during July 1940 as part of the shipping blockade. These had some success against seaborne targets.

One very successful E-4/B *Jabo* mission was an attack off Malta that sunk the Royal Navy ship HMS *Fuji*. Some *Jabos* were even adapted with a long, narrow tray that fit up to 96 antipersonnel "butterfly" bombs (SD-2s). These saw limited use against enemy concentrations, such as airfields.

As the Bf 109 itself improved with the succession of versions, so did production capability. As assembly lines multiplied from one to four, production jumped proportionately. Throughout most of 1938, when B, C, and D versions were produced, a total of fewer than 400 aircraft were built. With ample numbers of new DB engines, production of the Emil nearly quadrupled. The Emil's introduction came simultaneously with New Year 1939, and more than 1,000 were already built by August 31.

This would be dwarfed by wartime production, but in 1939 it was impressive. The transition was dramatic: in September 1938, one year before the launch of the blitzkrieg against Poland, the Bf 109 composed less than half the fighter strength of the Luftwaffe. At the time of the blitzkrieg's launch, the Luftwaffe had more than 1,000 Bf 109s operational. The *Gruppen* throughout Germany were poised to strike.

COMBAT PROVING GROUNDS

If the Spanish Civil War was the Messerschmitt Bf 109's combat testing ground, then the blitzkrieg of 1939 and 1940 would be its combat *proving* ground. The aircraft had reached a stage in development that matched or exceeded any fighter in the world. Learnings from Spain had matured the fighter to the technologically advanced E series.

The Emil had arrived in Spain just before *Legion Condor*'s withdrawal and didn't see combat action of any consequence. That would come soon enough—as Hitler's lightning strikes lit up the peaceful sky of Europe with breathtaking suddenness. These strikes would rely heavily on Emils to overwhelm enemy air power. Hitler first set his sights towards the east.

Poised for conquest, the Bf 109B-1 had seen action in Spain, but the Messerschmitt fighter would face much tougher opponents in the days to come. *Bowers Collection*

Bf 109 Numbers at the Outbreak of World War II

Luftflotte 1

I/JG 1	54 Emils
I/JG 2	42 Emils
I/JG 3	51 Emils
I/JG 20	21 Emils
I/JG 21	11 Bs and 18 Cs (29)
10. (*Nacht*)/JG 2	9 Cs
J.Gr. 101	36 Bs
J.Gr. 102	44 Doras

Luftflotte 2

I/JG 26	51 Emils
II/JG 26	48 Emils
I and II/ZG 26	57 Bs and 39 Ds (96)
10. (*Nacht*)/JG 26	10 Cs
J.Gr. 126	36 Bs and 12 Cs (48)

Luftflotte 3

I/JG 51	47 Emils
I/JG 52	39 Emils
I/JG 53	51 Emils
II/JG 53	43 Emils
1. and 2./JG 70	24 Emils
1. and 2./JG 71	21 Cs and 18 Es (39)
J.Gr. 152	44 Bs

Luftflotte 4

I/JG 76	49 Emils
I/JG 77	50 Emils
II/JG 77	50 Emils
I (*Jagd*)/LG 2	39 Emils
II/JG 186 (5. and 6.)	24 Bs
11. (*Nacht*)/LG 2	10 Emils
J.Gr. 176	25 Bs and 15 Cs (40)

Bf 109s Strike East

At 4:45 A.M. on September 1, 1939, Germany launched its attack on Poland to begin World War II. Participating were *Luftflotten* 1 and 4, commanded by General Albert Kesselring and General Alexander Löhr, respectively.

Luftwaffe pilots saw the first action of the war, as they flew through thick fog to reach interior targets about 15 minutes before the Wehrmacht's ground forces pushed east across Poland's border. Bf 109s flying in support of *Stukageschwadern* were among the first to fire in anger during World War II.

Germany's *blitzkrieg*, or lightning war, showcased the integration of a modern arsenal: a massive air assault

coordinated with a massive ground assault of tanks and troops. While ground forces consisting of motorized infantry and panzer divisions thrust toward Warsaw, elements of *Luftflotten* 1 and 4 thundered overhead in an array of aircraft: 648 He 111 and Do 17 bombers, 219 Ju 87 dive-bombers, 36 Henschel Hs 123 ground-attack planes, and 474 assorted reconnaissance and transport planes.

Spearheading them were the Luftwaffe's fighters. Although Bf 109s now numbered 1,000 strong, not even half were deployed for the blitzkrieg. Only 458 had been sent to the eastern airfields of Germany within the Bf 109's pouncing distance of Poland. The rest were kept in the west and throughout the interior in the event that British and French Allies lived up to their pledge to intervene if Poland were attacked.

Of the 458, the Luftwaffe actually sent only 215 Bf 109s on the initial strikes. There were also Bf 110 heavy fighters and even a few He 51 biplanes in the mix of fighters. Bf 109-equipped units participating in the opening attack were:

- I/JG 1 equipped with 54 Bf 109Es, all serviceable.
- I/JG 21 with both Bf 109Cs and Es, 29 total with 28 serviceable.
- J.Gr. 101 and 102 (soon to be redesignated II/ZG 1 and I/ZG 2 respectively, when transitioned to Bf 110s) with Bf 109Bs and Ds. J.Gr. 101 had 36 total, all serviceable; J.Gr. 102 had 44 total, with 40 serviceable.
- I (*Jagd*)/LG 2 with Bf 109Es, 39 total with 37 serviceable.

Note the mixture of B, C, D, and E versions. A lot of the older versions went into combat, while the greater number of new Emils were retained for home defense.

No matter which version of Bf 109 they faced, it was a losing game for the aircraft of the Polish Air Force. At

"Black men" pivot a Bf 109D-1 in ready position. *Black men* was a Luftwaffe nickname for the ground crews, because of their one-piece black cotton overalls. *Bowers Collection*

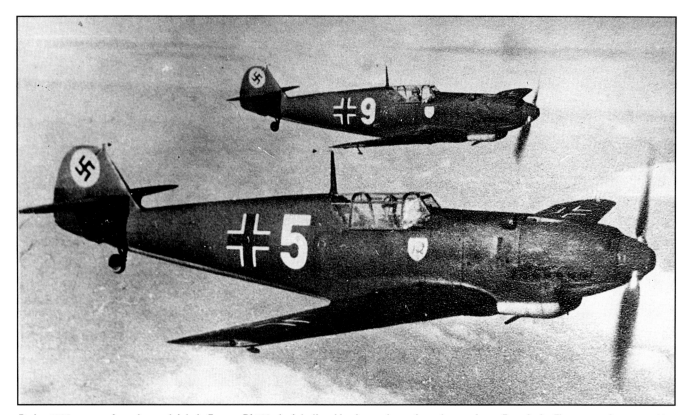

During 1938, a year of great uncertainty in Europe, Bf 109s took to the skies in greater and greater numbers. *Bayerische Flugzeugwerke* was working at full capacity and still not keeping up with Luftwaffe orders for C-1s, like these. Through licensing agreements, the Gerhard Fieseler factory in Kassel became the first to join in supplemental production of the Bf 109. *Bowers Collection*

most, Poland could muster 159 PZL P.7 and P.11 single-seat fighters in defense. The aircraft themselves were three to seven years old, and based on a design dating from 1931. Although this preceded Messerschmitt's creation (1934) by only a few years, the PZL's design was made instantly archaic by the Bf 109.

In addition to its fighters, Poland had 118 light bombers capable of an offensive role, 36 medium bombers, and 84 observation aircraft. Wehrmacht intelligence overestimated Poland's airpower, reporting 315 fighters, 325 reconnaissance planes, 150 bombers, and 50 naval aircraft.

While pure numbers of aircraft were overestimated, capabilities of the aircraft were accurately predicted: The Polish fighters' performance and armament were markedly inferior. The predominant frontline fighter, the high-wing monoplane PZL P.11, was hopelessly outclassed. Manufactured by Warsaw's *Panstwowe Zaklady Lotnicze* (National Aviation Plants), the P.11 couldn't attain equal altitude and was a full *100 miles per hour* slower than the Bf 109—slower even than the newer German bombers. Plus, most P.11s were armed with only two light 7.7mm machine guns. To make matters worse, only a small number had radios—a necessity in modern air battle where fighters had to be vectored to meet an oncoming threat.

Regardless of the mismatch, the Luftwaffe took the air threat seriously enough to give top priority to targeting

Polish airfields. The charge was to eliminate any threat from the skies for the advancing German ground troops. There was heavy cloud cover much of the morning on the first day. As skies cleared in the afternoon, the Heinkels, Dorniers, and Stukas, under the protective umbrella provided by both Bf 109 and 110 escorts, attacked Krakow's airfield. Other aircraft went on to pummel airfields near a half dozen other cities until runways became cratered ruins and hangars were ablaze.

Some Polish fighters had been rushed to secret alternate airfields in advance of the invasion. This saved the Polish Air Force from being annihilated on the ground, contrary to popular belief. From these secret fields, the Polish fighters operated early on to defend Warsaw, the Wehrmacht's ultimate objective. It became the job of Bf 109 pilots to find the fields and destroy them.

An early incident near Lodz tipped them off to the dispersal of aircraft. A *Jagdstaffel* bounced two Polish fighters and shot up both. Trailing smoke, one of them remained under control enough to descend in search of a place to land. The Bf 109s followed stealthily and thereby were led to one of the secret bases.

Eventually, other secret fields also were found and reduced to smoldering ruins, but not before 100 German aircraft of all types had been shot down in the first six days. If more of the available Bf 109s had been unleashed,

continued on page 49

COLOR GALLERY

After France fell in June 1940, the "black men" went to work repairing the ravages of aerial combat and preparing for continued conquest. The nearest Emil has wing cannons, but others do not. *Ethell Collection*

Nose of the Emil. The E-4 is the first version to have the heavier framed, square-cornered canopy (E-3s had a lightly framed, curved-glass canopy, common to all versions since the first prototypes). Plus, the E-4 has no nose-mounted MG FF cannon, which was tried and temporarily abandoned after problems in the E-3; hence, the E-4's closed-tip, pointed spinner. *Ethell Collection*

The hard-working ground crew of JG 53 fine-tunes this powerful Daimler-Benz DB 601. With aircraft flying from five to eight missions in a single day, the ground crew's work was never-ending. With the rapid succession of Daimler-Benz engines in the advancing Bf 109 versions, there was always something new to learn. *Ethell Collection*

After smashing victories over Poland, Norway, Holland, Belgium, and France, the Luftwaffe prepared for duty on the "Channel Front" in midsummer 1940. The paint scheme of the Bf 109E-3 shown here was the most common for Luftwaffe fighters during this period. *Ethell Collection*

With a backdrop of a Bf 109E, pith-helmeted members of JG 27 play a card game between sorties in North Africa. This Emil has been tropicalized for desert conditions, with a large air filter fitted on the supercharger intake along the port side of the nose. The filter was a rectangular box-like shape on Bf 109Es, but on later models it was a rounded canister. *Ethell Collection*

Gathered around their commander in front of his Bf 109E-3, these pilots look at maps for the day's mission. Mechanics bustle about behind, preparing the *Staffel* of nine Emils for a day of sorties. *Ethell Collection*

A Bf109F buzzes exhuberant colleagues cheering for the day's victories. *Ethell Collection*

In desert camouflage, a Bf 109E-4/Trop soars over the cool of the Mediterranean. This Emil pilot of I/JG 27 will soon descend back to the reality of heat and dust of the Libyan desert. While Rommel's Bf 109s often flew *Freie Jagd* over land to attack enemy troops, vehicles, and their fighter cover, some dogfighting over the sea occurred, especially as enemy or friendly supply convoys approached, and for attacks on the bastion of Malta.
Ethell Collection

Returning from a mission in his favorite Friedrich, *Hauptmann* Hans-Joachim Marseille shakes hands with a crew chief after another victory. Maybe *multiple* victories. Marseille once shot down six Curtiss P-40 Warhawks in 12 minutes over Bir Hacheim in June 1942. His marksmanship and control of his aircraft were extraordinary. (He wore tennis shoes while at the controls for surer feel of the rudder pedals.) Visible on his aircraft is the small triangular window just beneath the windscreen's oblique side window, installed through the Friedrich version, but not on Gustav.
Ethell Collection

An even dozen. Bf 109 victories came quickly during the blitzkrieg, while losses were few for the Luftwaffe. This German pilot puts the finishing touches on this day's victory—a stripe denoting a kill, crowned by a red star for the Russian aircraft he downed. *Ethell Collection*

The Bf 109 becomes a cash cow. As Germany felt a monetary pinch, it offered the Bf 109 for sale to select neutral and friendly countries. Among the first buyers in line were the Swiss. Knowing the Bf 109's capabilities after purchasing 80 earlier Emils (and a small number of Doras), the Swiss government secretly bought these Gustavs for home defense. They patrolled borders of Switzerland looking for aircraft of the Axis and Allied alike. Numerous other countries bought or were supplied with Bf 109s in various versions during wartime. Among them were Hungary, Yugoslavia, Bulgaria, Finland, Russia, and Slovakia (after Germany severed Czechoslovakia in two and made the Slovakian half into a satellite state). Japan also received two Emils, with the notion that native manufacturer Kawasaki could build a Japanese version, but Japanese pilots were not impressed with the aircraft, saying its high wing loading diminished maneuverability. *Ethell Collection*

Underside of an Emil with its unmistakable angular shape. *Ethell Collection*

A new Axis satellite receives fighters: Two Romanian Emils follow the lead of a German in the fall of 1942. The scene is befitting of the larger picture of Romania as a nation that willfully followed the lead of Germany. *Ethell Collection*

How many aviators can you fit on one Gustav? These young aviators of JG 53 repose on their aerial weapon. About the time it received this Bf 109F, JG 53 was based on the Foggia complex of airfields in Italy, which may be the setting for this photo. *Ethell Collection*

Ready for another sortie into the scud, a new Friedrich queues up on the tarmac behind an Emil. Subtle differences from the rear: The Emil has struts that angle up in support of the horizontal tailplane. The Friedrich has no external strut to brace its tail. Instead, its tailplane is cantilevered and positioned forward and lower than the Emil's tailplane. *Ethell Collection*

Three men who loom large in the Bf 109 story: Adolf Galland (center) and Werner Mölders (left) talk with the charismatic Ernst Udet. Udet, a World War I ace, was instrumental in selecting Messerschmitt's design in 1936 and later was head of the Luftwaffe's Technical Office, which oversaw production. Galland's and Mölders' exploits in Bf 109s made them famous in Germany and led to appointments to command posts. All three influenced the advanced development of the fighter. *Ethell Collection*

Once the terror of the skies, this Bf 109 is bent and broken at war's end. In the background is an He 111 in similar condition. *Ethell Collection*

In response to the RAF's "Window" that confounded German radar, the Luftwaffe turned to a lower-tech sort of defense: *Wilde Sau* (Wild Boar) Bf 109Fs like this were sent up to prowl the night skies for British bombers illuminated by searchlights and fires of burning cities. *Ethell Collection*

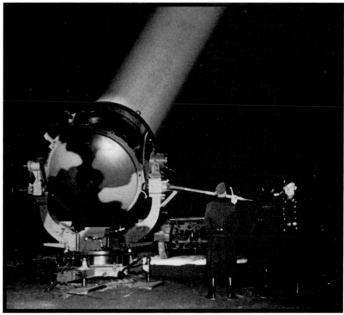

A few of the 33,000 Bf 109s built were kept intact and brought to the United States. One of the latest versions of the Bf 109 built during World War II, this G-10/U4 came to the USAF Museum in Dayton, Ohio, and was restored for display. It was built in Germany and believed to have been flown by the Bulgarian Air Force during World War II and later the Yugoslavian Air Force. As displayed, it has an Erla Haube canopy and drop tank. *USAF*

The HA-1112-M1L, a Spanish-built version of the Bf 109, approaches Steve Wittman Field at Oshkosh, Wisconsin. *Dennis Sherman*

Once on active duty with the Spanish Air Force, this HA-1112-M1L has markings of 71 *Escuadron* of *Ala* 7 *de Cazabombardeo*. It carried the number C.4K-100, now C.4K-19 and nose art "Mapi." *Author's Collection*

Pilots appreciated that the Bf 109's gauges were simple and logically arranged, and that controls were close at hand. Although cramped, the layout of the cockpit is sparse and purely functional—all built around two devices: the reflector gun sight (at the top of the instrument panel, its lenses aligned for viewing out the windscreen) and the firing buttons at the top of the "joystick" or control column. This Bf 109G-10/U4 cockpit has been meticulously restored, along with the rest of the aircraft, by Evergreen Aviation Educational Center. *Brian Silcox*

In his painting *The Gustavs' First Pass*, Mike Zimmerman recalls a Bf 109 attack on a formation of B-17s over Germany. Following a common tactic, the Bf 109s have come from a position of 12 o'clock high, diving through the formation with cannon and machine guns blazing. They then wheeled around for another pass.
Mike Zimmerman

Painted in accurate colors, the engine of the G-10/U4 is displayed. The Daimler-Benz DB 605D inverted V-12 engine with 1,450 takeoff horsepower made it the fastest of the Gustavs. Top speed was 426 miles per hour (at 24,280 feet). The aircraft is exhibited at the USAF Museum in Dayton, Ohio.
Author's Collection

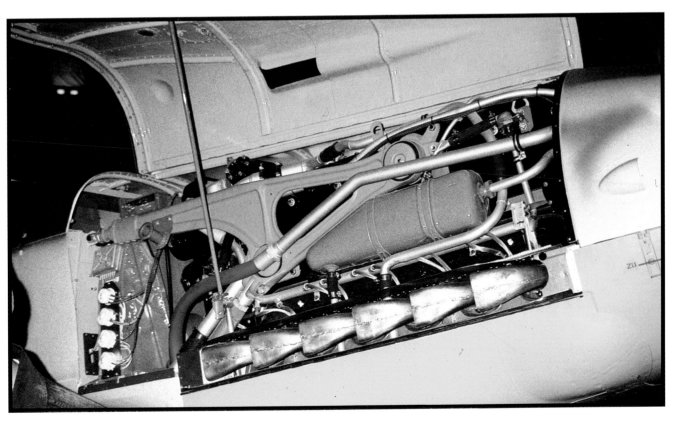

The HA-1112-M1L's Rolls-Royce Merlin engine caused a slightly swollen nose shape. This resulted in its nickname, *Buchón,* for the puffy-chested pigeon common to Spain. Note the four-blade propeller (versus the three-blade propeller of the Daimler-Benz). *Author's Collection*

Continued from page 32

far fewer of the German bombers would have been lost, but Germany could not gamble with its home defenses.

Even the seasoned veterans of *Legion Condor* were surprised by the ferocity of the Polish pilots. Pilots of the tiny PZL fighters hurled themselves into German formations, tenacious to the absolute limits of their aircraft. Some resorted to ramming the German aircraft in defense of their homeland, but the skill and equipment of the German pilots would prevail.

Poland's "Pursuit Brigade," consisting of five squadrons under direct control of the Supreme Commander of Polish Forces in defense of Warsaw, was crushed by September 17. With its demise, the Polish Air Force no longer existed. It was also on September 17, in Poland's most desperate moment, that Russia invaded from the east, accelerating Poland's inevitable collapse.

After this, German air supremacy was so complete that Bf 109s were no longer needed for the escort role. Bombers flew unescorted over Warsaw, pulverizing it into rubble. Even lumbering Junkers Ju 52s (trimotored transports that stood no chance against any opposing fighter) flew unescorted, dropping explosives at random out of side cargo bays onto the helpless city.

Bf 109 units switched from an air-to-air role to air-to-ground attacks in direct support of the advancing German divisions. It was in the ground-attack role that 48 Bf 109s were lost during the four weeks of September. Twelve downed Bf 109s had been claimed as Polish fighter victories, and seven more were claimed by bomber gunners, for a total of 67 Bf 109s lost by the end of the campaign.

Following Poland's capitulation, the Luftwaffe continued its transition to the Bf 109E in the remaining fighter units, while the B and C models were relegated for use as trainers in the *Jagdfliegerschulen* (fighter pilot school) and remaining D models were transferred to duties with the *Nachtjagdstaffeln* (night fighters).

The Phony War

A by-product of the German invasion of Poland was the "Phony War." The Germans called it *Sitzkrieg* (Sitting War). Britain and France had paid lip service to their pledge of support to Poland by declaring war on Germany on September 3, 1939. But little action followed, at least on the ground. Ground troops were indeed "sitting" in this phony war. Ground forces of both sides remained static—the Germans safely behind the Siegfried Line and the French behind the Maginot Line. But for Bf 109 pilots, there was nothing phony about the air war.

Bf 109s patrolled the frontier's airspace, encountering Allied aircraft including French Amiot 143s and Farman 222s on reconnaissance missions, and shooting them down (I/JG 3's Werner Mölders, with 14 victories the top-scoring

A British Vickers Wellington made it out of German airspace—by just a few feet—after a decisive Bf 109 and Bf 110 attack. Twelve such bombers had attacked the German Navy near the estuary for the Elbe River—the beginning of a few sporadic encounters in what came to be called the Battle of Heglioland Bight. Through the attacks, the British learned that bombers shouldn't fly without fighter escort in daylight. The Germans did not take note of the lesson, and suffered because of it in later offensives. *National Archives*

ace in the Spanish War, flew his Bf 109 to another 9 victories this way by May 1940).

There were losses on the German side, too, that became a treasure for Allied aircraft designers. At the end of September 1939, a Bf 109E flown by *Unteroffizier* Georg Pavenzinger of 2./JG 71 was forced down near Nancy. The *Unteroffizier* was taken prisoner and his aircraft was taken for testing by the French (it later crashed in testing). Another Emil, this one flown by *Feldwebel* Karl Hier of 1./JG 76, landed on November 22 at Worth in bad weather. It was later turned over to the British for testing.

After two costly and ineffective raids in September,[8] RAF bombers returned on December 14 to attack the German fleet. Twelve Wellingtons roared toward the German Navy bases just north of the estuary of the Elbe River. *Major* Harry von Bülow's II/JG 77 shot five of them down.

On December 18, 22 RAF bombers materialized again over the Bight in daylight, flying in wing-to-wing formation in an approach toward Wilhelmshaven, where numerous German capital ships were anchored. Heavy antiaircraft fire forced the bombers to take violent evasive action. As the bombers banked northwest in search of refuge, they came nose to nose with their worst nightmare—a *Jagdgeschwader* of Bf 109E-3s. These fighters from JG 1, along with Bf 110s, ravaged the formation, sending them spiraling down into the North Sea. In all, 12 of 22 Wellingtons were destroyed with a loss of two Bf 109s and three pilots wounded.

Bf 109s Strike West

Early on the morning of April 9, 1940, the Phony War ended decisively when Germany invaded Denmark and Norway to secure its northern flank. German victory came with relatively little help from the *Jagdgeschwadern*. The Luftwaffe's role in both countries was primarily bombing and ferrying paratroops and Alpine troops in Ju 52s.

Low-flying Bf 109s flew overhead at Copenhagen, more as a show of force than anything. With 15,000 troops and only a token air force, the Danes surrendered with little resistance.

Bf 109s saw little more action in the primarily seaborne invasion of Norway. Only II/JG 77's 30 Bf 109E-3s participated. Fighter pilots who hadn't seen action over Poland anxiously expected a challenge, but found little to satisfy them. Bf 110s of I/ZG 76 had been given responsibility for eliminating the Norwegian Air Force's 100 fighters and reconnaissance aircraft, leaving the Bf 109s little to do. Some RAF aircraft were dispatched to help, but these were mostly Blenheims, Sunderlands, and Hudsons with no fighter escort due to lack of range. Bf 109s intercepted them over the sea and picked them off easily.

If the British and French counterattack had included air power, more Bf 109s would have been called in. As it was, both Allies sent expeditionary forces but a deliberate decision kept their aircraft at home, because there weren't enough for home defense, let alone operations in Scandinavia.

A collection of downed RAF Fairey Battles. Once the RAF's great hope as a first-line strike bomber, the Battle was rendered obsolete largely by the performance of the Bf 109. Originally faster than most fighter aircraft, the Battle could neither get away nor defend itself from intercepting Bf 109s. There were over 1,000 in RAF service in 1940, and 10 squadrons of them deployed to France during the "Phony War." In May, when Germany attacked France, the British sent them up against marauding Bf 109s. Slower and feebly armed, with only a single Browning .303, the Battles were slaughtered. By the end of 1940, the survivors were pulled from combat units. *National Archives*

On May 10, 1940, the Germans invaded the Low Countries "to protect these neutrals from Allied aggression," in Hitler's convenient reasoning. In reality, Hitler pounced on Holland, Belgium, and Luxembourg as a first step toward his long-anticipated attack on France. Against what everyone knew would be stiffer opposition, the Luftwaffe unleashed many aircraft—about 3,500 in total. Of these, 850 were Bf 109E-3s from JG 2, 3, 26, 27, 51, 52, 53, and 54. The fighters had dual roles: bomber escort and free-chase sorties.

Opposing them were *De Luftvaartafdeling* (Dutch Air Force) and *L'Aeronautique* (Belgian Air Force), along with the French *L'Armee de l'Air*. The Dutch mustered a total of 124 aircraft, among them enough fighters for four fighter squadrons. These were equipped with 28 Fokker D XXIs, as well as 23 Fokker G1As and a few Douglas DB8s.

The Belgians had similarly modest numbers. Among 157 aircraft were 78 fighters that included 13 Gloster Gladiators, 11 Hawker Hurricanes, 24 Fiat CR 423s, and 30 Fairey Foxes.

The French fighter forces numbered as many as 828 aircraft, but only 584 were serviceable on May 10. The French fighters were divided into 23 units, called *Groups de Combat*. Four of the groups flew Curtiss Hawk 75As, the only foreign-built fighters imported in time to face the onslaught. The Hawk 75 was a capable fighter by standards of the time, but was clearly inferior to the Bf 109E-3. Other French units flew Morane Saulnier MS 406s, Bloch 151s and 152s, Potez 630s and 631s, and the Dewoitine D520. Packing the punch of two 20mm cannons and two 7.5mm machine guns, the Bloch 151s and 152s had comparable armament to the E-3. These were powered by a 1,080-horsepower Gnome-Rhone engine, capable of propelling the somewhat ungainly fighter at speeds of 323 miles per hour.

Before the invasion, the RAF had sent contingents to help: two squadrons of Gladiators and four squadrons of Hurricanes. Immediately after Germany launched the blitzkrieg westward, the RAF sent another six squadrons of Hurricanes.

Still, the Luftwaffe outnumbered all opposing air forces combined. Not only did it have the advantage in numbers, but in unity of command and advanced planning. The opposing air forces were fragmented, under

Hermann Göring awards decorations after successful campaigns in the East and West, at a time the Luftwaffe seemed invincible. Göring had said that his air force was ready to "execute every command of Der Führer with lightning speed and unprecedented might." For the moment, his boastful harangue seemed to hold true. *National Archives*

separate commands and struggling with the problems of communication—both in the physical network and native tongue. (German ground forces of two million soldiers were massed on the western border, but these were slightly outnumbered by the combined Allied ground forces.)

Ignoring the "invincible" Maginot Line, the Germans simply skirted its northern end or flew past it. In the same pattern as the invasion of Denmark and Norway, the vanguard of German troops—both paratroops and airborne infantry—were delivered by Ju 52s.

Objectives for air attack were clearly identified. Initial targets in Belgium were the large fortress of Eben-Emael and the bridges of the Albert Canal where it intersected with the Meuse River. In the Netherlands, objectives were to capture intact the Rhine bridges at Moerdijk and Dordrecht and the capital city of The Hague. Beyond that, airfields were first-order targets of destruction in each country, particularly the French air bases at Lyon, Romilly, Dijon, and Nancy. Bf 109s flew the usual escort for Stukas and horizontal bombers.

At the aforementioned bridges, where panzer units and motorized infantry needed to cross, Bf 109s had the reverse role of *protecting* sites on the ground. As a defensive measure, the Allies frantically tried to destroy the bridges by sending a succession of bomb-toting British and French aircraft, including Blenheims and Fairey Battles, Breguet 693s, and Amiot 143s. These were not well suited to the ground-attack role, nor did they stand a chance against attacking Bf 109s. Fairey Battles in particular took a beating from Bf 109s, dispelling the RAF's great prewar faith in them. Flying continuous patrols from dawn to dusk, Bf 109 pilots warded off the attackers and in the process ran up their victory scores while suffering practically no losses.

Without Bf 109s in the escort role, *De Luftvaartafdeling* and *L'Aeronautique* had some success in damaging or downing Ju 52s and bombers, but both air forces were quickly whittled down to handful of surviving fighters within a few days. When the Netherlands surrendered on May 14, only five Fokkers remained. Belgium hung on longer, until May 28 when its air force was completely knocked out and its ground forces had suffered heavy casualties.

Now, in the pattern of the Polish blitzkrieg, rampaging Panzers struck a wedge into the flank of France as they raced toward the Atlantic coast. Overhead, Bf 109s repelled every major air-to-ground assault and cleared the way for the advancing Panzer divisions. Seemingly omnipresent and invulnerable, Bf 109 pilots chalked up victory upon victory. On May 12, a young pilot named Günther Rall of 8./JG 52 scored a victory—the first of 275 total. On May 14, 90 Allied aircraft were shot down near Sedan—39 of them claimed by JG 53 alone. On May 17, 1./JG 3 downed an entire formation of Blenheims near St. Quentin without a single Bf 109E lost. By then, German armor was advancing so fast that the biggest challenge became the fighter's short range, because forward airfields could not be set up fast enough to keep pace. German supply lines had been stretched taut and logistics were becoming a challenge. Spare parts were lacking and fuel was sometimes short.

In the hands of skilled pilots, the RAF's Hurricanes and French aircraft scored victories on occasion, but the Luftwaffe's superiority was clear from the outset. Even as the Allies fought bravely in the air, their ground-based counterparts were losing ground so rapidly now that they found no friendly base to return to. Many aircraft were lost on the ground, too, either being captured as bases were abandoned or destroyed by German aerial attack.

The successful air and ground offensive was driving Allied ground troops back toward the northwestern coast, namely Dunkirk. On May 24, 1940, Hitler ordered the advancing German columns to halt. This was when the garrulous Göring made his famous boast—one of several in World War II that would later haunt him—that "the Luftwaffe alone could finish off" the Allied armies at Dunkirk. A subsequent boast: "If the Allies ever bomb Berlin, my name is Meyer." He soon was known as "Meyer" to a lot of Berliners.)

The very first of the Bf 109-Spitfire clashes took place about this time in the vicinity of Dunkirk. On May 23, an RAF squadron commander downed over France had evaded capture and was hiding near Calais. To rescue him, a two-seat Miles Master trainer was sent, along with two Spitfire I escorts. The British account is that, after they'd picked up the squadron commander, the three aircraft were jumped by 12 Bf 109s as they attempted to flee back to the safety of England. The Spitfires downed three and damaged two, and went on to escort the two-seater back. It's possible that the claims

A terrifying sight that sent enemy troops running for cover on the ground: an Emil thundering overhead. *National Archives*

were exaggerated in the melee of combat, but the encounter was foreboding: Bf 109 pilots experienced for the first time a formidable adversary who could fight on equal terms.

More encounters with Spitfires followed in the coming days, as the Allies tried to buy time for their trapped troops. In a series of small-scale confrontations, fighters lost were about the same for both sides.

Assuming that the several hundred thousand Allied soldiers were cornered helplessly at Dunkirk, Göring was slow to act. He didn't know that the British were already assembling a huge, ragtag fleet that would number 887 rescue boats. Just as he was about to unleash the Luftwaffe's full fury, the weather turned. Beginning the night May 27, and continuing through May 31, a downpour grounded the Luftwaffe.

On June 3, the Luftwaffe took to the air again with waves of bombing raids that leveled aircraft factories and smashed airfields, while the panzers resumed their advance. On the following day Dunkirk fell, but not before the incredible happened: 338,226 soldiers had been evacuated, about two-thirds of them British and the rest Dutch, Belgian, French, Polish, and Luxembourgers.

Elsewhere, the German advance surged on. On June 6, Werner Mölders, commander of III/JG 53, was shot down near Chantilly. Mölders had been downed by a 24-year-old Frenchman named Pommier Layrargues. Mölders later asked to meet the pilot who had beaten him, but Layrargues had been killed moments after the victory when three other Bf 109s closed in on him.

Paris was occupied on June 14. And by June 19, work was over for the Bf 109 in the Battle of France. On June 22, six weeks after the start of the invasion, the French signed an armistice.

Losses of aircraft had mounted for both sides. France's air fleet was neutralized. And although Great Britain lost 509 fighters in the last 40 days, few had been Spitfires. Those had been prudently held in reserve for defense of the British Isles. The great majority lost were Hurricanes, which showed vulnerability to the Bf 109E—surprising and perhaps shocking to Hawker engineers, but not to Willy Messerschmitt. Bf 109 losses numbered less than 200.

With victory won, captured German pilots were now released from prisoner-of-war (POW) camps. Among them was Mölders who, like many Luftwaffe pilots, could have been transferred to an interim camp in England and ultimately sent to Canada. His release placed another natural-born pilot and marksman back into the seat of a Bf 109.

All along the French coast, directly across from England and separated by as little as 20 miles, the Bf 109s, along with Stukas, Heinkels, and Dorniers, commandeered new home airfields—some no more than flat avenues of grass; others were long-established and had relatively luxurious accommodations, freshly vacated by the *L'Armee de l'Air*. The Bf 109's limited range required them to have the airfields nearest the coast directly opposite Great Britain. *Luftflotte* 2 carved out new strips near Wissant and Cap Griz-Nez, Coquelles, Audembert, and Marquise. *Luftflotte* 3 took home fields used previously by *L'Armee de l'Air* at Maupertus, Dinan, Querqueville, and Guernsey, and set up new grass fields at Crepon, Carquebut, and Plumetot.

A break in the action gave time to evaluate the E-3 further. Enhancements were made both on the production lines and through retrofittings in the *Jagdgeschwadern*. Several changes improved protection and visibility of the pilot: Eight-millimeter seat armor, weighing 53 pounds, was installed, along with a 28-pound curved plate attached to the hinged canopy. Plus, the "square" canopy came into being with its heavier framing that afforded better visibility by repositioning the framing away from eye-level. An appreciated side benefit was more headroom. The MG FF cannon also was upgraded to fire improved ammunition, and armament advancements led to redesignation as the E-4 (see chapter 3). Cannon upgrades to the existing inventory of Bf 109s in line units in effect turned E-3s into E-4s.

Werner Mölders scored 25 victories before the Battle of Britain (including 14 during the Spanish Civil War). He had been shot down during the Battle of France, and spent a short time in a prisoner-of-war camp before France and Germany arranged an armistice. After his release, he resumed blazing a remarkable trail of victories in Bf 109s. For his piloting prowess, he was appointed *Kommodore* of JG 53 at the age of 27. Although he was extremely young for the position, he showed such uncommon maturity that men of his *Jagdgeschwader* called him *Vati*, or "Daddy." *National Archives*

Prelude to the Battle of Britain

As the Battle of France was cooling down, the "Battle over the Channel" was heating up. The objective of this battle was simple: To stop all shipping across the English Channel. By Hitler's direct order, the responsibility for the blockade fell heavily on the Bf 109 units. Any Allied ship was a target. This Channel activity overlapped with the Battle of France, since the attacks against shipping began when reinforcements and supplies began arriving from Great Britain.

Throughout the summer, the aerial attacks on all cross-Channel shipping persisted as weather permitted. The Spitfires held in reserve during the Battle of France were now unleashed in defense of the Royal Navy and merchant marine. As a result, many of the Luftwaffe's vulnerable bombers were shot down, but losses mounted for both sides. The Channel campaign cost the Luftwaffe 286 aircraft, including 105 Bf 109s and Bf 110s; it cost the British 148 Spitfires and Hurricanes.

The Luftwaffe had gained mastery of the air from the moment it took to the skies over France and the Low Countries, and for the six-week blitzkrieg following. That never quite happened over the Channel.

Clearly, an effective strategy for an attack on Channel shipping had not been carefully thought through from the beginning, and the Luftwaffe's pilots knew the bitter taste of failure for the first time. Also clear was the fact that the RAF was a much tougher adversary than expected.

The *Jagdgeschwadern* were reequipped over the ensuing weeks. Bf 109s were serviced and many retrofitted with the latest advancements. New pilots were mixed in with the old salts.

There was an ominous lull, as Great Britain faced the real possibility that it could be invaded. The English Channel was the age-old protection between them and the new mechanized divisions that had rolled across Continental Europe, but the Channel would not slow down the Luftwaffe. In London, Winston Churchill tried to rally his beleaguered nation. At that moment, Great Britain stood alone., and the Battle of Britain was about to begin.

CHAPTER 4

BF109S IN THE BATTLE OF BRITAIN

A UGUST 13, 1940. FROM REICHSMARSCHALL GÖRING TO ALL UNITS OF LUFTFLOTTEN 2, 3, AND 5: ADLERANGRIFF. WITHIN A SHORT PERIOD YOU WILL WIPE THE BRITISH AIR FORCE FROM THE SKY. HEIL HITLER.

With that order, the massive aerial assault code-named *Adlerangriff* (Attack of the Eagles) against England was supposed to begin. But its beginnings did not live up to the glory of its name. It would not end gloriously for the Luftwaffe either.

It had all the makings of a classic contest, however, like a boxing match between two world contenders. The "contenders," in this case, were the single-engined fighters of Great Britain and Germany—the Spitfire and Hurricane versus the Bf 109. Later, Winston Churchill himself would summarize the rivalry of the aircraft by saying: "The Germans were faster with a better rate of climb; ours more maneuverable, better armed." From a technological point of view, it was an even match.

There was a lot of attention given to the tiny fighters, during the battle and since. Of course, it wasn't supposed to be that way. From the point of view of both the Luftwaffe and the RAF, this wasn't a showdown of fighter aircraft. The sole aim of the Luftwaffe was to get its bombers with their deadly payloads over the target, and the RAF was bent on stopping them. In Hitler's words delivered personally to Göring: "Bombing (not dogfighting) would destroy the . . . ground organizations and supply installations

A *Schwarm* of four Bf 109E-3s from 7./JG 51 during 1940. Materializing above the English Channel, wave after wave of formations like this roared overhead in the coastal area of Dover on their way toward London and RAF fighter bases ringing it. Once over London, the Emils had at most 20 minutes of fighting time before they had to turn toward home for lack of fuel. The return was often the most harrowing leg of the trip, as pilots clung to the hope of making it back across the Channel after the red fuel-warning light came on. *Bowers Collection*

of the RAF and the British air armaments industry." Then the land invasion code-named Operation *Seelöwe* (Sea Lion) could commence and, like all other invaded countries so far, Great Britain would surely fall to its knees.

More than British freedom hung in the balance. America was teetering between remaining isolationist or entering the war. So, the Battle of Britain became also a fight to win the sympathies and support of the United States.

British victory showed the Americans, who didn't like Hitler but didn't know what could be done about him, that Nazi Germany wasn't invulnerable and that Great Britain *did* have a chance—with U.S. help. In this way, the Battle of Britain took on epic proportions. Although there were ramifications in a far larger context, it *did* boil down to a showdown of fighter planes and their pilots. It's why Germany's Messerschmitt Bf 109 and Great Britain's Spitfire and Hurricane became synonymous with the Battle of Britain.

"Still Churchill's Channel"

As the two sides strapped in for aerial battle, fighter numbers were comparable: 832 British fighters of both types, Spitfire and Hurricane, would be pitted against 878 Bf 109Es. These Bf 109s were from two air fleets, *Luftflotten* 2 and 3, which were dispersed across bases mostly in newly won France. *Luftflotte* 5 was a new air fleet created in Scandinavia; since its Bf 109s did not have long enough range to operate across the North Sea, they had no part in the battle.

The Bf 109s were supplemented with about 320 Bf 110s that would prove to be of little value. All these were to protect the waves of bombers sent to blast England's defenses to oblivion.

Hitler demanded in his fateful Directive No. 17 that the Luftwaffe was to vanquish the RAF "with all means at its disposal and as soon as possible," as a means to clear the way for invasion of the British Isles.

The objectives for the Luftwaffe were clear:

1. To blockade the British Isles (along with the German Navy) by attacking ports and shipping, and mining of sea lanes and harbors.
2. To win complete air superiority by sweeping away all RAF fighters.
3. To pulverize the British into submission through massive bombing and neutralize all remaining defenses.

Göring was sure he'd make short work of the RAF. And he had good reason to believe he could. While playing a major role in the blitzkrieg, his Luftwaffe had overcome all challenges presented by the now-occupied countries. Even the capable air force of France had been soundly beaten. The Bf 109 *Jagdgeschwadern* and the Luftwaffe as a whole had no equal—no opposing forces had even come close. The pilots were undeniably the best trained, equipped, and most seasoned of any air force, bar none.

To top it off, extensive intelligence reports, called *Studie Blau*, or Study Blue, had been prepared with utmost confidence by the intelligence section of the *Oberkammando der Luftwaffe*. The fact was that, during July 1940, the British produced 496 Spitfires and Hurricanes, while the Germans produced only 220 Bf 109Es—meaning German output was less than half of the British. But *Studie Blau* only showed pronounced inferiorities and crippling vulnerabilities of the RAF.[9]

Truly believing that he'd gain complete air superiority with laughable ease, Göring assured his *Führer* that all airborne defenses would be eliminated within 13 days after *Adlertag* (Eagle Day). The launch date for *Adlerangriff* was now set for August 10, 1940. And certainly the air war would be won before Operation *Seelöwe*, set for September 15, a full six weeks away.

But a week before *Adlertag*, the Luftwaffe had already suffered a blow. In a single afternoon, JG 27 lost nine Bf 109Es in a debacle on August 8. The mission that day was routine: attack Channel shipping. General Wolfram von Richthofen ordered the attacks against a convoy of about 20 ships. Low cloud cover—barely 2,000 feet—left precious little headroom for Stuka dive-bombing. Conditions were so poor in the morning that the Luftwaffe returned to base frustrated. There was little damage done to the convoy.

In the afternoon, conditions improved somewhat. Von Richthofen dispatched about 30 Bf 109Es and a small number of Bf 110s, along with three *Stukageschwadern*. British radar registered a strong blip signifying a large formation of approaching enemy aircraft and scrambled about 35 Spitfires and Hurricanes to take up station over the convoy.

As Galland said, "[The Stukas] attracted Hurricanes and Spitfires as honey attracts flies." But the ensuing battle was textbook perfect for the Luftwaffe: The Bf 109s held their adversaries at bay, allowing the Stukas to dive-bomb their seaborne targets. Although the Stukas swooped down to a greeting of barrage balloons and anti-aircraft fire, four ships were sent to the bottom and others damaged. The Germans returned to base after this success, but von Richthofen still wasn't satisfied.

He ordered a force more than twice the size to finish off the convoy. The Luftwaffe struck again with success, leaving only 4 ships out of 20 to reach England's shore. But this time, the RAF came in greater force. The adversaries clashed in a ferocious battle that sent the Luftwaffe packing. That's when the RAF's "legless legend," Wing Commander Douglas Bader, radioed a terse message home: "It's still Churchill's Channel."

Downed that afternoon were 60 German aircraft, according to exuberant RAF pilots. Luftwaffe records later revealed an exaggeration: About half of that—31 German planes—had been downed that day, 9 of them Bf 109s.[10]

With this clash over the Channel, the RAF marked August 8, 1940, as an official beginning to the Battle of Britain.[11]

All things considered, the Bf 109 and British Spitfire, as shown here, were very evenly matched during the Battle of Britain. The Spitfire I had a Rolls-Royce Merlin II liquid-cooled V-12 engine with 1,030 horsepower, capable of attaining 362 miles per hour in level flight at an altitude of 18,500 feet. The E-4 could achieve 357 miles per hour at 19,700 feet. *National Archives*

Adlertag: Aerial Attack Sputters to Life

When August 10 came, foul weather precluded launch of the onslaught. August 11 was little better and only a disappointing few raids were flown. Still nothing to be heralded as *Adlertag*.

On August 12, *Erprobungsgruppe* 210 took to the sky to strike its first land target. It was to be a preparatory strike against British radar, so that *Adlerangriff* would have a chance of surprise. Eight Bf 109E-4/B *Jabos*, along with 12 Bf 110s also equipped as fighter-bombers, bore down on the radar antennas of the Kent and Sussex coastal areas. The experimental group's pilots found their targets—spindly 350-foot masts—and dropped their bombs. All around the masts were explosions that destroyed attendant structures. But after the last bomb fell, they saw that the masts still stood. Once home again, they learned through detection devices that the radar stations resumed radar operations within a few hours. Even well-placed bombs had not been able to bring down the antenna towers themselves.

Finally, on Tuesday, August 13, with sky-high hopes, Göring sent the order quoted at the beginning of this chapter. *Adlerangriff* would wipe the RAF from the sky.

But it would not go as planned.

A succession of human errors started the Germans off on the wrong foot, which seemed to set the rhythm for the prolonged months to come. To begin with, the German weathermen botched the forecast: Instead of "a high pressure zone over the Azores ensuring a few good days," as confidently predicted, there was steady drizzle and a thick cloud blanket over the Channel. That was confirmed early enough, in predawn weather reconnaissance by a Dornier Do 17, to alter plans.

Göring himself sent word that the mission would be postponed until afternoon. All Bf 109 units stood down, but word did not reach some other units. The illustrious *Adlertag* sputtered to life in the form of abortive sorties of a *Geschwader* of bombers that had not received the postponement order. Seventy-three Do 17 "flying pencils" sallied forth alone to their target at Eastchurch, which intelligence identified as a fighter airfield. (In fact, it was not a fighter airfield but instead a Coastal Command base.) Ten of 73 bombers were shot down and more would have been lost had it not been for the cloak of cloud cover.

Göring reset launch time for *Adlertag* to 2 P.M. that same day, but the weather deteriorated even further. The Luftwaffe launched in mass anyway. There were more misadventures—sorties over England in which crews couldn't find their targets in the scud and returned to base with their bombs still aboard. Other flights of Stukas and Bf 110s were bounced by Spitfires resulting in German aircraft shot down.

Late that afternoon the Luftwaffe finally managed a successful raid. A *Jagdgeschwader* of about 100 Bf 109Es escorted a formation of Stukas to attack the airfield at Detling. There, the Bf 109s engaged awaiting Spitfires, while the Stukas successfully bombed the field. Many airfield buildings and 22 parked aircraft were destroyed. But later, the Germans realized that Detling was not a fighter base—it was a Coastal Command base like Eastchurch—with no Spitfires or Hurricanes stationed there.

By the end of the day, it was clear that the "onslaught" of *Adlertag* was actually more like a pinprick. The Luftwaffe returned dismally to its bases with 46 total aircraft lost. Only 13 Spitfires and Hurricanes had been shot down. A total of 47 British aircraft of various types had been destroyed on the ground, but not one of the RAF's fighter bases—the primary targets—had been seriously damaged.

No knockout punches delivered. It was as if two boxers had exchanged only glancing blows, then returned to their corners. And now the two stood stunned and looking warily at each other from across the Channel. If the Luftwaffe couldn't pack more of a punch than this, Britain had little to fear.

What the Bf 109 pilots and Luftwaffe leadership couldn't know at this time was that, with *Adlerangriff*, they now had been committed to an exhausting, punishing battle—a battle of attrition which the Luftwaffe, like the Third Reich as a whole, could not sustain. Losses would be devastating.

Pilots like Ulrich Steinhilper, a Luftwaffe ace from JG 52, saw firsthand the danger signs of "a war of attrition, an airborne version of the dreadful trench warfare of 1917–1918. Sooner or later one side had to run out of aircraft and young men to fly them." For many young Bf 109 pilots, such dim prospects for survival led to debilitating fatigue and stress called *kanalkrankheit* (channel sickness). Steinhilper explained, "At first there were isolated cases but, as the battle dragged on, there were to be more and more cases of the evil disease. The symptoms were many and various but surfaced as stomach cramps and vomiting, loss of appetite and consequently weight and acute irritability. Typically the patient's consumption of alcohol and cigarettes would increase, and he would show more and more signs of exhaustion. There was little leave and, unlike the RAF pilots, we were not to be circulated to a quiet zone for short periods of rest and refitting."

The foul weather of *Adlertag* left aircrews groping in the soup. This crew races to the awaiting Heinkel He 111 for a bombing mission to England. The He 111's service closely paralleled the Bf 109's, seeing combat first in Spain. The He 111's operational life also would be prolonged by Spain's aircraft builders after the war. *National Archives*

Tethered by Short Range, Tethered to Bombers

Coastal radar installations remained primary targets for a time, but additional bombing proved futile—little better than *Erprobungsgruppe* 210's first attempt. *Oberst* Paul Deichmann, chief of staff of *Fliegerkorps* II, scoffed at the effort, saying to leave the radar alone. "Let the radar do its work so they can find our fighters," he said. "They will deliver themselves for destruction." Before the end of August, the primary targets shifted to inland fighter bases, mainly those ringing London.

With the concentration on inland targets, the Bf 109's problem of short range became acutely apparent. With an operational radius of only 125 miles, Bf 109s were like attack dogs on short leashes.

The Bf 109 units closest to London were located at Calais. A roundtrip from Calais to London left only 20 minutes of dogfighting time before Bf 109 pilots *had* to return. If they didn't, they couldn't count on making it back. After the red fuel-warning light came on, they had perhaps a nerve-racking five minutes to find a place to land. Often the light came on just as the English coast passed beneath them. Pilots then had a choice of dropping to sea level where wind resistance might be lower, or climbing for enough altitude to glide the distance back to French shores once fuel was gone. It was a life-or-death gamble either way.

After pancaking a Bf 109 or parachuting into the frigid Channel, a pilot couldn't hope to survive more than a couple of hours before succumbing to exposure or drowning. The Luftwaffe had an air-sea rescue service, but pilots were hard to locate and many Bf 109 pilots died waiting. Ulrich Steinhilper later wrote:

We couldn't leave the bombers because they were being constantly harassed by enemy fighters and so the object became to conserve fuel as much as possible. However, it isn't easy to fly straight and level and give proper protection, so the precious fuel reserves were soon running low.

The fighters held their positions, and as we began to cross the Channel we could see that the bomber force was still intact. Now it became a fight for survival for the fighters. At last we could break away and we all dropped virtually to sea level where the wind resistance is lower. We literally wave hopped, hoping that our fuel gauges were wrong, and that we would just have enough to get to France. One after another our comrades came on the radio to report that their red fuel-warning lights had come on. Below us we could see the gray, uninviting waters of the Channel with waves running very high. We knew that if we tried to land the aircraft in such rough water our chances of survival were slim. So as fuel ran still lower the orders were to try to gain a little height and jump, at least this gave an improved chance of survival, although not much better.

One after another the fighters plowed into the waves of the channel or rose in a last desperate search for height before the pilot bailed out. Our track across those wild waters became dotted with parachutes, pilots floating in their life jackets, and greasy oil slicks on the cold water showing where another 109 had ended its last dive. Our air/sea rescue people tried their best, but it was so hard to locate the men in the high waves. Most that were located were already dead, victims of exposure or drowning. The next day I was privileged to see a secret memorandum which reported 19 pilots drowned. In all, only two were recovered by the *Seenotflugkommando*.

My group of four survived and had just made it to Boulogne where we refueled. All along the coast near Boulogne we had seen 109s down in the fields and on the grass, some still standing on their noses. The losses to us had been huge. When we four flew into our base the ground crews went wild with joy. . . .

It was a major oversight that a practical Bf 109 drop tank had not been perfected prior to the Battle of Britain. He 51s had carried them already in the Spanish Civil War. Stukas had them, too. The tank available for Bf 109s at this time was made of plywood, and leaked like a sieve.

Bf 110s had the range, but it was due largely to their failure in combat that Bf 109s were called upon to fly beyond reasonable range. Messerschmitt and his engineers had designed the twin-engined Bf 110 *Zerstörer* (destroyer) as a strategic fighter. In theory, the long-range Bf 110 was to sweep ahead of the bomber formations, coaxing RAF defenders in to the air, then clearing the way. Even if the Bf 110s were not able to shoot down the defenders, the theory was that the Spitfires and Hurricanes would be forced to return to base to refuel and rearm. In the meantime, the bombers would roar past to their targets. Then the Bf 110 would join the bombers as escorts home.

In practice, the scenario did not play out even remotely like the theory. Despite high speed and powerful armament, the Bf 110 fell as easy prey to both the Hurricane and

Immediately recognizable by its elegant elliptical wings, a Spitfire banks below a Dornier Do 17 over Southeast England. Like all German bombers, the Do 17 needed Bf 109 escort for survival. *National Archives*

Spitfire. The smaller single-seaters were infinitely more agile and made short work of the Bf 110s (usually before fuel shortage became a concern), then the British fighters would go on to intercept the unescorted bombers. During August 1940 alone, 120 Bf 110s—a devastating 40 percent committed to *Adlerangriff*—were shot out of the sky. The Bf 110 would later find good use as a night fighter, but in the Battle of Britain, the Bf 110 seemed like a hopeless cause. Ironically, to fly with any degree of safety, a Bf 110 required escort by Bf 109s!

As a result, Bf 109s were needed as escort for virtually every aircraft. Suddenly, in orders from the very top, Bf 109s were relegated strictly to a supporting role as escorts. As German cities now became targets in British night bombing missions, Hitler became completely obsessed with reprisal bombing.

With this order, the Bf 109 had its wings clipped a few weeks after *Adlertag*. Previously, the fighter had enjoyed the dual duties of both bomber escort and *Freie Jagd* (free hunt) to seek and destroy at will. But henceforth, the Bf 109 was no longer to range freely using the tactics best suited for its design. Instead it was to fly only close escort missions, tight at the side of the bombers striking the inland bases.

Galland protested, "The fighter must seek battle in the air," reiterating the words of Manfred von Richthofen, the fighter legend from World War I. Von Richthofen had said, "Fighter pilots must be free to rove . . . in any manner they wish, when they wish. And when they find the enemy, they *attack* . . . anything else is rubbish."

With bombing as the top priority, more Bf 109s were given the assignment as *Jabos*. One *Staffel* in each *Gruppe*

RAF veteran Richard Townshend Bickers notes in his book *The Battle of Britain* that 1,172 RAF fighters were downed from July to October 1940—most "fallen to the guns of the Messerschmitt single-seater." During the same period, 610 Bf 109s were lost. Ulrich Steinhilper, JG 52, described the experience of shooting down a Spitfire: "I began to position *Yellow 2* [a 109E-4]. The red ring of the Revi gunsight was projected onto the windscreen, and I'd already flipped the trigger for the guns over to be ready with both the nose guns and the cannon in the wings. Gradually the Spitfire filled the ring of the sight and I increased the pressure on the triggers. Four lines of tracer hosed out toward the target and I saw strikes, the aircraft spinning away." *National Archives*

was ordered to equip its aircraft and train its pilots in the fighter-bomber role. Following methods developed by *Erprobungsgruppe* 210, a thin red line was drawn at 45 degrees on the side glass of the canopy as an aid for the "bombardier" (the reluctant pilot) to help him align with the horizon. The bomber role was *not* welcomed by fighter pilots who, in practice, often ditched their bombloads at the first opportunity.

In time, the Luftwaffe's focus on the inland RAF fighter bases was actually achieving the desired big-picture effect. A half-dozen fields around London, in particular Biggin Hill and Manston, had been bombed severely and were barely operational. More RAF fighters were being shot down or blasted on the ground than could be replaced. The Germans knew it, because fewer and fewer Spitfires and Hurricanes now rose up to intercept the incoming Luftwaffe formations.

But, as Luftwaffe ace Heinz Knoke wrote in retrospect: "Again and again the German High Command believed that the last of the doggedly fighting Spitfires must have been shot down. Yet again and again, as the days become weeks and the weeks become months, our bombers and fighters were still being engaged in combat by more fighters taking to the air, undaunted by the large numbers of the RAF who crashed to their deaths every day."

Comparisons Between Opponents

Many comparisons have been drawn between the German and British single-engine fighters. It seems everyone had an opinion, and not all so objective as Winston Churchill's, stated earlier. Adolf Galland had his, too.

The problem with fuel: You couldn't put enough in. Short-legged Bf 109s with an operational radius of only 125 miles strained to get back to their bases day after day. At this point in the war, there was ample fuel, but the number of aircraft was short. Later in the war, the two factors would flip-flop. *Bowers Collection*

He deftly dismissed the Hurricane by saying, "The Hurricane was hopeless—a nice airplane to shoot down." RAF pilot Al Deere pointed out that the Hurricane was superior to the Spitfire as a gun platform that had greater effect on bombers, "but it could not have lived without Spitfires to take on the 109s, whereas the Spitfires could have lived without the Hurricanes."

Obviously, complicating factors make comparisons difficult between the Bf 109 and its British rivals. For example, tethering Bf 109s to bombers kept them confined, as did inadequate fuel capacity that often forced them to withdraw even though circumstances favored them. The British, too, broke off aerial engagements at times for lack of fuel, but more often because they had to pursue the target of Luftwaffe bombers.

It also depended on tactics. The Luftwaffe was able to polish its tactics in the Spanish Civil War; the RAF hamstrung itself by clinging too long to the old tight "vic" or "three-finger formation" originated for biplanes, until it was forced to imitate the success of the Luftwaffe's *Rotte*, or pair, formation of a lead ship and wingman.

Between the two British fighters, the Spitfire has been judged most like the Bf 109. Differences between the Spitfire I and Bf 109E were marginal, difficult to quantify,

and more difficult to prove. Comparing strictly facts, armament differed. The Bf 109E had two cowl-mounted Rheinmetall-Borsig 7.92mm machine guns and two wing-mounted MG FF 20mm Oerlikon cannons. The Spitfire (and Hurricane) had eight wing-mounted, Browning .303-inch (7.7mm) machine guns. The RAF determined that the cannon was better than machine guns, so cannons were tested during the Battle of Britain, but were problematic. They were abandoned for the time being and weren't used again until well after the Battle of Britain.

The RAF's machine guns had a rate of fire of 1,200 rounds per minute; the Bf 109's machine guns 1,100. The Spitfire carried 300 rounds for each of its eight guns; the Bf 109 carried 500 rounds in the nose for each of its cowl-mounted guns. The Bf 109E's cannon carried 60 explosive shells.

For a powerplant, the Bf 109E had the Daimler-Benz DB 601A inverted V-12 rated at 1,150 horsepower; the Spitfire had the Rolls-Royce Merlin engine rated at 1,020 horsepower. The fuel injection of the DB 601A was a definite advantage over the Merlin's carburetors, since fuel injection enabled Bf 109 pilots to invert or abruptly dive. With a carburetor, the inverted attitude would cause the engine to sputter and lose power unless the pilot was able to half roll and thereby send a surge of fuel into the en-

typical airframe won't break up until upward of 9 Gs or more). For lack of instruments at this time, the pilot could do nothing but rely on "gut feel" to stay within survivable stresses for his airframe.

One finds as many opinions about flying and fighting characteristics as authorities. For characteristics like climb rate, radius of turn, and even top speed, there are disagreements, all spoken with supreme confidence. However, there are many governing factors, such as altitude and atmospheric conditions (i.e., at some altitudes the Bf 109E was faster; at others, the Spitfire I was faster). Certain facts came out of testing at R.A.E. (Royal Aircraft Establishment) Farnborough: Because of the Bf 109's higher wing loading, it had a wider turning circle than the Spitfire. Both fighters seem to have had aileron heaviness at high speed, but R.A.E. pilots identified this as the Bf 109's biggest disadvantage: aileron heaviness prevented a fast rate of roll in a high-speed dive.

An objective assessment came in wartime, when a captured Bf 109E-3 was tested in the spring of 1940. Comparisons to the British fighters are implicit:

Good Points

a. High top speed and excellent rate of climb.

b. Good control at low speeds.

c. Gentle stall, even under *g*.

d. Engine did not cut immediately under negative g.

Bad Points

a. Controls, particularly the ailerons, far too heavy at high speeds.

b. Owing to high wing loading, the airplane stalled readily under G and had a poor turning circle.

c. Aileron snatching occurred as the slots opened.

d. Quick maneuvers were difficult at high speed because of (a) and at low speed because of (b) and (c).

e. Absence of a rudder trimmer, curtailing ability to bank left at high speeds.

f. Cockpit too cramped for comfort when fighting.

Armorers of 8./JG 51 load 7.92mm ammunition for this Bf 109E-3's Rheinmetall-Borsig MG 17 machine guns. Meanwhile, life imitates art: *Staffel* 8's arch-backed black cat emblem has a match on the cowl. *Bowers Collection*

gine (certainly not a fine point that a pilot wants to deal with in the mayhem of dogfighting when every second counts and any movement might mean the difference between life and death).

The Bf 109 had a constant-speed propeller, which the Spitfire did not have initially. The RAF recognized a need for them through tests of captured Bf 109s, eventually installing them on Spitfires. By August 15, the new constant-speed propellers replaced fixed-pitch or two-pitch props on almost all Spitfires. Constant-speed propellers improved performance, like increasing service ceiling, and also reduced wear on engines.

For structural durability, the Spitfire was praised. It stood up extremely well to high stress, but if too much stress was exerted, the Mitchell wings could fold. The Bf 109 had similar weakness in the wings, but weaker still was the tail, which was supported on struts (a pilot may black out at stresses as low as 4 Gs, while a

Hopeful he won't need it this day, a JG 51 pilot straps on his parachute during the Battle of Britain. Like all *Jagdgeschwadern* participating in the Battle of Britain, JG 51 was located at an airfield near France's coast. Most forward bases were nothing more than commandeered pastures. *Bowers Collection*

As quickly as this JG 51's 109E-3 can be rearmed and refueled, the pilot climbs in for another mission. Within a moment after the canopy is closed and chocks are pulled, this fighter will be rocketing down the grass strip. At the end of August 1940, just before the Luftwaffe went on an all-out at-tack against the RAF fighter arm, Major Werner Mölders took over command of JG 51 from Major-General Theo Osterkamp. This was about the same time that a half-dozen other young fighter pilots took over *Jagdgeschwadern* commands, including Major Galland, who took command of JG 26. A great competition began between *Jagdgeschwadern* to be top scorer of *Adlerangriff*. Such exuberant aspirations would give way to desperation, as the Battle of Britain turned disastrous for the Luftwaffe. *Bowers Collection*

Ulrich Steinhilper gave this objective comparison for later models introduced during the Battle of Britain: "This was the time of the arrival of the Merlin XII engine fitted with the two-stage supercharger and the Mk. II Spitfire. The first of these were issued to 61 Squadron on August 22, 1940, and 195 of them had entered service by the end of October. They not only gave an improved rate of climb and speed but also an improved service ceiling. The Me 109E-4 was being fitted with the DB 601E engine, which improved the power by 100 horsepower over the N engine. This gave improved performance, but it was not keeping up with the Mk. II Spitfire, the engine of which had its output increased from 1, 030 horsepower to 1,150 horsepower. This increased the speed and gave a huge advantage in service ceiling. The Me 109E-4 was capable of reaching 10,000 meters (32,800 feet) with the Mk. I Spitfire reaching a comparable 10,363 meters (34,000 feet). But the new Mk. IIs soared up to 11,340 meters (37,200 feet), giving a tactical advantage of 1,340 meters or 4,300 feet to the Spitfires."

Whether the Bf 109 or the Spitfire was the "better" aircraft has been hotly debated ever since the Battle of Britain. In the final analysis, the outcome probably rested in the ability, confidence, and aggressiveness of the pilot.

Withdrawal

As fall 1940 dragged on for the Luftwaffe, it was becoming clear that Great Britain would not "be brought to its knees" through aerial attack, as Hitler counted on and Göring assumed. The German High Command realized in early October, as winter closed in and days got shorter, that the Luftwaffe could not win the battle of attrition. Hitler postponed Operation *Sea Lion* indefinitely and eventually abandoned it. By the end of October, the Battle of Britain was officially over.

Overall, the Luftwaffe failed to achieve its objectives in its air campaign. But it did not fail all aspects of it: The Messerschmitt Bf 109 held its own in the battle of the fighters.

Göring changed his strategy to night bombing, pummeling Great Britain from Portsmouth in the south all the way to Glasgow, Scotland, in the north, with primary focus on London. Night bombing would continue through May 1941. But even before the end of 1940, the Bf 109 units were withdrawn from the western coast and brought home. In Germany, the *Jagdgeschwadern* were given R & R and reequipped with the newest version of Bf 109s to face a new opponent—the juggernaut in the east, the Soviet Union.

Bf 109E-3 Specifications

Dimensions—Wingspan: 32 feet, 4 1/2 inches. Length: 28 feet, 4 1/2 inches. Height: 8 feet, 2 1/3 inches.

Weight—Empty: 4,189 pounds. Loaded (at takeoff with fuel, pilot, and ammunition): approximately 5,875 pounds.

Powerplant—Daimler-Benz DB 601Aa fuel-injected, inverted V-12, liquid-cooled engine. Takeoff horse-power: 1,100.

Armament—Two 20mm Oerlikon MG FF cannons, mounted in the wings; one 20mm Oerlikon MG FF engine-mounted cannon (this cannon was eliminated in the E-4 version); two 7.9mm Rheinmetall-Borsig MG 17 machine guns, mounted above the engine.

Performance—Maximum speed: 348 miles per hour at 19,700 feet. Maximum range: 410 miles on 88 Imperial gallons of fuel (106 U.S. gallons). Maximum rate of climb: 3,280 feet per minute.

Spitfire I Specifications

Dimensions—Wingspan: 36 feet, 10 inches. Length: 29 feet, 11 inches. Height: 12 feet, 7 1/2 inches.

Weight—Empty: 4,517 pounds. Loaded (at takeoff with fuel, pilot, and ammunition): approximately 5,844 pounds.

Powerplant—Rolls-Royce Merlin II supercharged, liquid-cooled V-12 engine. Takeoff horsepower: 1,020.

Armament—Mk. I: Four .303 (7.7mm) Browning machine guns. Mk. IA: eight .303 (7.7mm) Browning machine guns. Mk. IB: two 20mm cannons and four .303 (7.7mm) Browning machine guns. All were wing-mounted.

Performance—Maximum speed: 355 miles per hour at 19,000 feet. Maximum range: 450 miles on 85 Imperial gallons of fuel (102 U.S. gallons). Maximum rate of climb: 2,420 feet per minute.

CHAPTER 5

PILOT TALK: GERMAN

THE FOLLOWING PILOT RECOUNTS ARE EXCERPTS FROM OTHER PUBLICATIONS (AS NOTED) AND DIRECT QUOTES FROM INTERVIEWS.

Hans-Werner Lerche: Luftwaffe Test Pilot

It was known that at takeoff and landing the Bf 109 always kept some unpleasant surprises in store, not only for pilots flying it the first time, but also for experienced veterans. Basically, the powerful engine combined with the small airframe favored a tendency to swing to port at takeoff, while at landing, if leveled off a little too high above the ground, the 109 had a habit of suddenly dropping a wing—the after-effects of which could not be prevented by the narrow undercarriage. But if one did not make any howlers, the Bf 109 could be flown quite safely. When our routine program called for 100-hour endurance tests with this fighter, I was able to make two flights in the Bf 109F-4 CF + BN. For my third flight I was to take the Bf 109G BD+LF in a climb to its operational ceiling. According to my instructions, at takeoff and immediately afterward the new DB 605 engine was to run first with emergency power and then at combat power in a climb to the ceiling. At first all went well, but at 10,500 meters (34,450 feet) the engine started misfiring. After testing both magnetos I knew that it had nothing to do with ignition. As I was not keen on waiting until the engine caught fire, I immediately discontinued the flight and landed safely. It was known that a fire in the Bf 109 could be most unpleasant, especially for a beginner in fighter testing. As it turned out, my action was fully justified—there would have been

The standard Luftwaffe-issue flight book. These recorded far more combat hours than their average Allied counterparts. While British and American pilots eventually had a system of quotas to complete a tour, German pilots were expected to fly missions until they were shot down and killed or captured. *Author's Collection*

a fire, as an examination of the engine proved later on: one cylinder, or rather the piston, had refused to grind on and demonstrated this by punching a sizable hole in the piston head. In those days, it seems, this phenomenon was not all that rare with this engine.

Having thus proved an "old hand" at flying fighters, I was given the chance of flying the Spitfire IIA, then just completing its evaluation at Rechlin, together with its 1,200-horsepower Rolls-Royce Merlin engine. It was intended to make some flights for filming purposes, in which I was to simulate a crashing Spitfire by means of an attached smoke cartridge.

The first thing I noticed was that, when taxiing, the field of vision was not as good as in the Bf 109 because of the "wide shoulders" of the 12-cylinder upright-V engine. To make sure not to overrun somebody, one had to work vigorously with the pneumatic brake lever at the control column and with the rudder pedals to advance in snaking lines. The takeoff and flying the Spitfire were not difficult: It was sensitive in the elevator, but the stick forces for the ailerons were rather high, especially when diving. Thanks to its armament and the low wing loading, the Spitfire was a remarkable opponent in climbing and turning dogfights, but I think at that time it was a little slower than our fighters. It is well known that the Spitfire was continually improved in turn with the German fighters, and therefore an exact comparison of their performance could only be made with regard to given altitudes and taking into consideration the continuous changes of the engine power, airframe, and armament. Above all, there would have been no point in comparing the latest German types available at Rechlin with the captured Allied aircraft, which had been in service for some time. (Excerpt from *Luftwaffe Test Pilot* by Hans-Werner Lerche. Jane's Information Group Ltd. © 1980.)

Ulrich Steinhilper: Bf 109 Pilot, JG 52 (Piloting *Yellow 2*, a Bf 109E-4)

I felt the gentle rocking of the aircraft as [mechanic Erwin Frey[12]] began to wind up the eclipse starter . . . turning over the big DB 601 engine. I pulled for the start, she roared into life immediately, and I set the throttle lightly forward so that I could complete my after-start-up checks. All eight remaining Mes were running now at their different dispersals, and we began to taxi out for takeoff. . . .

Glancing around me, I pushed the throttle to full power and felt the aircraft accelerate, the tail coming up almost immediately. Bumping over the rough field, we bounced a little and I felt her become light as we lifted clear of the earth. Retracting the gear, I waited just a few moments while the air-speed increased, then eased back with the stick and we were climbing away nicely. The churning in the stomach had stopped now; everything was under control. Check the positions of the other aircraft. Begin to tighten up into formation for the climb. . . .

We would assemble and set course for London. The British radar would pick us up as we assembled over France and set course. As we began our flight, the British pilots would still be taking tea, waiting for the word. As we crossed the Channel they would scramble and climb to their service ceiling, ready to pick us up as we approached London. They would follow us, waiting with the advantage of height and speed, then, as we began our turn for home, both at the tactically weakest spot and at the extreme of our range, they would peel off and hell would break loose again. . . .

"Out of the sun! Out of the sun!" The warning broke through the babble of voices and static on my headphones. I looked back over my shoulder and saw my faithful wingman, *Feldwebel* Schieverhöfer, flying exactly where the sun was brightest. He had heard the warning and stayed flexible, diving below me and coming up on my left side. I made a steep turn, full throttle, rudder bar hard round and the stick against my leg, the engine turning at 2,800 rpm—400 too many! We had to make as much speed as possible—the British fighters were diving toward us.

. . . Schieverhöfer and I took up our positions in the classic *Rotte*, ready to protect each other's tail when necessary. We'd got some way behind the formation and unless we could make up the distance, we'd hang like ripe plums in the sky. Then the curt warning came again. "Out of the sun! Out of the sun!" Four or five of the Spitfires

dived toward Schieverhöfer. My little finger found the radio button on the stick and I pressed it as I shouted the warning, "Lother! Watch it!" I made to turn to protect his tail, only to see him turn protectively toward me. Instead of diving away he was turning to shoot behind my tail. I glanced back into the glaring light and there, behind me, was a staircase to the sun. A staircase of Spitfires queuing for the attack. The first one already had red flames dancing along the leading edge of the wings as his guns fired.

. . . We were fighting for our lives now and both of us would have to act alone. I dived away and saw that the engine was now turning at 3,300 rpm, the throttle fully open. I couldn't risk the engine blowing up, so at 7,000 meters (22,000 feet) I leveled out. Up until then, I hadn't been hit or so I hoped. Further down there was a layer of cloud which would hide me on the next dive, I made for the sanctuary.

I was taking stock of my position when—*Bang!* — there was an explosion at the left side of my fighter, near to the front. The control column shook as something hit the elevators in the tail. For a moment I thought that I had been hit, but a search of the sky revealed no enemy aircraft. "It must be the supercharger," I thought. It turns at about 10 times the speed of the engine, and I had badly overrevved that in my attempt to escape the attack by the British fighters. The supercharger had probably exploded owing to the overrevving, with pieces of it hitting the control surfaces as they passed to the rear. It didn't look as if it was going to be my day.

I checked the instruments and controls to see if there was any obvious damage. All seemed to be working, but I was losing oil from the damaged supercharger. The loss of the charger also meant that I would have to fly lower to get power from the engine. My airspeed was about 700 kilometers per hour (400 miles per hour) in the dive and I was still weaving from left to right, both for protection and for better observation. I put the nose down and glided toward the cloud layer below

Leutnant Ulrich Steinhilper. In the hangar behind is one of JG 52's Emils that saw action in the Battle of Britain. *Peter Osborne*

Werner Oest, center under spinner, stands with others from JG 301. Established in September 1943, this night-fighter unit was initially based in Bavaria, where Oest joined it. The unit would distinguish itself in both daylight and nighttime missions. *Werner Oest*

at about 2,000 meters (6,000 feet). Once inside the milky soup of the cloud I relaxed a little and the control column eased back. In moments I was out in the blinding brightness of the sun, it pained my eyes but at least I was able to check my course. With constant side-stepping and weaving, my compass was running wild and I needed the sun for a definite fix. My experience of this route told me that the sun should be ahead and slightly to the right, and I was reassured to see that my course was about right. There I let the aircraft slide back into the anonymity of the clouds.

Now I had real trouble. I looked at the temperature gauge with horror, it was just passing 130 degrees C. Why? I knew that the engine was probably losing oil from the damage to the supercharger, but that wouldn't account for the abnormal temperature of the coolant. There was only one conclusion—I had been hit during the attack—probably in the radiator. . . .

Slowly I had reached 2,000 meters again, still within the cloud base. My speed was down and so I decided to give the aircraft a rest, I even talked to it. "Now my *Yellow 2*, see how carefully I will treat you, I will even turn your ignition off, so you don't burn your insides out.

Then I was down to 500 meters (1,600 feet) and began to attract some light antiaircraft fire. I could see a small town, but did not recognize it. Now: ignition on. The propeller was being constantly turned by the airflow, so there was no problem in restarting the engine. Soon I was

gaining height and the oil temperature stayed within limits. Just before I entered the cloud I transmitted a better fix for the ground station, telling them that I would fly a fixed course of 100 degree magnetic. It would all help them to find me in the water. So far so good, the engine was running very well, no special noises and adequate power. But, the oil temperature began to rise as I watched it. As I reached cloud base I noticed 100 degrees C and rising. There was only one sensible thing to do, cut the engine and glide again. As I glided down I could see what I thought was the Bay of Manston (Pegwell Bay) and I gave this as my new position. . . .

The engine fired quickly but after a few moments it started to run very rough. I eased the throttle back as much as possible but with so little power I could barely maintain height. My heart thumped against my ribs and I sweated in spite of the freezing October temperatures. Even with a minimum throttle setting, the engine cried out in pain—it was now metal on metal. How long could this last? A last hope. Full throttle—would it help? It certainly did—the engine seized!

There was no "bang" or disintegration of the engine parts, just a soft silence. I had never known this before in a 109—just the whistling of the wind as it passed at about 220 kilometers per hour (140 miles per hour). There was only one choice now—jump. A last desperate radio message: "From *Eule* 2a—engine seized—bailing out." The message sounded ridiculously loud in the quiet of the cockpit. It was fantastic how many thoughts went through my mind a few seconds; "Should I try to land? No! I must destroy my aircraft. It must not fall into enemy hands." I ran through the emergency procedures in my head: Oxygen equipment off. Throat microphone off. Remove flying helmet with headphones. "Poor *Yellow 2,*" I thought, "This is your last moment." I pulled the lever to jettison the canopy. All that happened was that the knob came off in my hand and the release lever wouldn't move any more. I glanced at the altimeter—only 250 meters (800 feet) now—I must hurry. There was only one choice, open the canopy as normal. This would allow me to get out, but the rear section would stay in place. I pulled the lever and pushed up on the perspex. There was a sudden explosion of wind noise as loose items were sucked out of the cockpit by the slipstream. I gasped as freezing air poured into the aircraft. The canopy was wrenched from my hand by the air pressure and torn off the hinges. I heard it rumble down the side of the fuselage before it fell into the void below.

Now it was my turn. Release seat belts and push up into the gale which was buffeting my body. Suddenly, disaster. The slipstream had forced my body backward, wedging my parachute under the rear section of the canopy. My legs were jammed under the instrument panel and I was being bent backward. I tried to claw my hands down toward the control column to bring her up into a stall but I could not reach. To my horror I saw the aircraft begin her last dive. Slowly she rolled to the right and the nose began to drop into a critical dive. There was only one option for me now. I had to risk tearing my parachute pack. I leaned out to the right and with huge effort I pulled my legs up toward my body. Suddenly I was out and rolling along the side of the aircraft—even at only 200 kilometers per hour (125 miles per hour) you are the victim of a powerstorm. I somersaulted, head over heels and hoped that with luck I would pass the tail without injury. After a second I was clear . . . I saw my brave *Yellow 2* diving toward some soft ground in the middle of a herd of cows. They scattered in all directions, running with their tails up. Then there was a soft thump as she entered the ground, and the 20mm ammunition started to go off immediately, a kind of ridiculous last salute. (Excerpt from *Spitfire on My Tail,* by Ulrich Steinhilper and Peter Osborne. Independent Books © 1989.)

Werner Oest: Bf 109 Pilot, JG 301

I flew Fw 190s in 1943. I also flew Ju-87 Stukas, dropping bombs. But most of my hours were in Messerschmitt 109s.

Many of our missions were night missions. JG 301 was a night-fighter group based in Munich. But we also often flew day missions. A memorable one was in 1944. It started the usual way. The mechanics crawled up on the right wing with the heavy starting handle. They wound up the inertia starter as I sat ready in the cockpit with the

Werner Oest mounts his Bf 109 as dusk nears. *Werner Oest*

canopy open. I closed up and off I went. Every fighter pilot in the area was being scrambled.

The Allies were attacking Berlin with 600 aircraft en route. Every able pilot from JG 301 was flying from Munich to Berlin to help. We had to fly there from way in the southern part of Germany to the far north, fight in combat, and fly back.

We flew at our normal altitude of 9,000 to 10,000 meters on the way. As we were approaching, I could see many Flying Fortresses. They were all in good formation ahead of us, passing left to right at lower altitude. We had a magnificent view of them.

Our eyes scanned above and below for American escorts. We saw nothing but an endless procession of American bombers with their long, long vapor trails marking their route from the west. We curved to the right, racing parallel with them to get into attack position.

We dove at them at full throttle. You could hear the 109's distinctive whine as we gained speed. The American gunners opened fire with all they had as soon as they saw us. We waited until we were closer, then fired bursts from our machine guns and cannons. We watched our tracers streaking toward them, then we saw the flashes as they struck the wings and other upper surfaces. With a sky so full it was almost difficult to miss.

A blink of an eye later, a number of the bombers burst into huge fireballs, as bombs intended to explode on the ground in Berlin exploded in midair instead. There were many gaps now in their formation. We saw the sky start to fill with parachutes and debris.

Meanwhile, flak started exploding around us as we had now descended to 4,000 or 5,000 meters. Our own flak batteries were shooting at us. Their officers didn't expect us to enter into the field of fire of their 88mm guns to mix with the Americans. Two from my squadron were shot down this way and both pilots parachuted safely. I was not hit.

That day, I shot down a B-17, but it has been credited only as a probable.

Later in 1944, I flew 109s as escort for Junkers Ju 88s for three weeks. I crash-landed once because of engine problems. I crash-landed another time—shot down by a Spitfire. I bellied in near Munich on April 27, 1944, at 3:45 A.M.

I shot down one Spitfire, too, which would seem to support the belief that the fighting qualities of both were nearly equal. In total, one Spitfire I shot down was confirmed, two were probables.

Against the British fighters, the best thing about the 109 was that it could fly inverted and make sharp turns. But it couldn't climb as fast. With the Daimler-Benz motor of more than 2,000 horsepower, it was superb at low altitude. The Spitfire was better for stalling and handling at high altitude. The Fw 190 gave more trouble to the Spitfires and other Allied fighters because it had better weapons and generally was a newer, faster design.

I won't say the 109 was a joy to fly, but I loved flying, I was motivated to fly. Luftwaffe pilots all were grounded after the war. No more flying. No more Messerschmitts or any other aircraft. When they finally lifted the sanction in 1955, I was the 14th to be relicensed as a pilot in Germany.

Heinz Knoke: Bf 109 Pilot, JG 52

Log entry for February 28, 1942: "Suddenly I tense inside. There he is, just a few feet overhead. A Spitfire. The RAF roundel markings are the size of cartwheels.

The Supermarine Spitfire, because of its maneuverability and technical performance, has given the German formations plenty of trouble. "*Achtung*—Spitfire!" German pilots have learned to pay particular attention when they hear this warning shouted in their earphones. We consider shooting down a Spitfire to be an outstanding achievement, as it certainly is.

With a jerk I lift the nose of my plane. I have to get him!

But by now he has spotted me also. He whips around in a tight turn toward me, drops his nose, and straightens out in a dive far below.

Throttle back: bank to the left. I must not lose sight of him. With both hands I pull the stick back hard into my belly while in a vertical bank; my body feels as if a giant hand is pressing it down into the seat, and for a moment my vision blacks out.

There he is again. He had put his plane into a vertical dive and is heading west for the open sea. I go down in a dive after him. At full throttle the noise of the engine becomes a frenzied scream, and the vibration causes the wings to quiver under the strain.

I adjust the sights and fire.

Must get closer range. To gain increased speed I close the radiator cooling flaps. Never mind if the radiator boils over; never mind if the engine goes to pieces—I have to get him, whatever happens.

The Spitfire goes down like a meteor shooting through space. That plane is certainly a magnificent piece

A Bf 109E in *Freie Jagd* looking for trouble. Note the bulges on underside of wings for the 20mm MG FF cannons. The wings were so sleek and slender that breeches had no where to go but out—in the form of a *buele*, or bulge panel, added to allow room. *Bowers Collection*

of work, and it is being flown by a lad who knows what he is doing and has plenty of nerve.

- 20,000 feet: he is in my sights, and I again open fire.
- 18,000 feet: range is too great, estimate at 1,000 feet.
- 12,000 feet: my engine is beginning to boil.
- 10,000 feet: the dive is now even steeper than before.
- 6,000 feet: the Spitfire is faster. The distance between us increases. My eardrums are popping, and my head feels like bursting. This vertical power-dive is hell on a pilot. I have ripped the oxygen mask from my face. There is an overpowering smell of glycol. The engine has boiled. The oil temperature rises. Still the airspeed indicator registers over 500 miles per hour.
- 3,000 feet: slowly the Tommy straightens out from the dive. We both skim low across the snowfields in the high coastal mountains.

This Spitfire is a terrific plane. The gap between us widens steadily. We reach the open sea.

I give up the chase. My engine is about to seize. Throttle back; open the radiator flaps. My Tommy is now no more than a tiny speck on the horizon.

(A few days later, on March 5, 1942, Knoke has another chance at what he believes is the same Spitfire.)

Ahead and to the left I discern a tiny dark speck in the sky against the unbroken white landscape below.

It is the Spitfire, leaving a short vapor trail behind . . . over his objective, the Tommy flies round in two complete circles. He is taking photographs.

I make use of this opportunity to take up a position above him . . . I am now about 3,000 feet above him.

Then he starts back on a westerly course. I open my throttle wide and check my guns as I swoop down upon him. In a few seconds I am right on his tail. Fire!

My tracers vanish into his fuselage. And now he begins to twist and turn like a mad thing. Must not let him escape. Keep firing with everything I have.

He goes into a dive, then straightens out again. He begins trailing smoke, which gradually becomes denser. I fire yet again.

Then something suddenly splashes into my windshield. Oil. My engine? I have no visibility ahead, and am no longer able to see the Spitfire. Blast!

My engine is still running smoothly. Apparently the oil in the front of my eyes must have come from the badly damaged Spitfire when its oil cooler was shot to pieces.

I veer a little to the right, in order to be able to observe the Tommy farther through the side window. He is gradually losing speed, but is still flying. The smoke-trail is becoming thinner.

Then another Messerschmitt comes into view climbing up on my left. It is Lieutenant Dieter Gerhard, my old comrade, and I radio him to say that I am no longer able to fire.

"Then let me finish him, Heinz!"

He opens fire. The right wing of the Spitfire shears away. Like a dead autumn leaf, the plane flutters earthward. (Excerpt from *I Flew for the Führer*, by Heinz Knoke. Greenhill Books © 1997.)

Wilhelm Stoll: Stuka Gunner

When a Messerschmitt took a direct hit on its wing, there was no chance for the pilot to bail out. I watched in horror numerous times when a 109's wings were broken off this way and the aircraft would spiral down—the pressure pinning the pilot in his seat.

When hit in the tail, the Messerschmitt nosed down and dropped like a stone. I watched one start to fall, then shatter totally into pieces. Again, no chance for the pilot.

The Messerschmitt 109s were, of course, much faster and more maneuverable than Stukas. But they were not safer. They needed a longer runway than a Stuka, so we took off from separate bases and met up en route to target.

My last flight over Stalingrad was my most memorable. There had been many victories for the Messerschmitts over the Yaks. But this time we encountered heavy flak. I watched as flak struck one 109 escort. Its gas tanks exploded in a great flaming burst and it crashed without the pilot getting out.

You get emotional for a moment, knowing that a good pilot was just lost. You feel thankful it didn't happen to you. But you don't want to spend time thinking about it. You focus on what you're supposed to do. And you focus on survival. Most of all, you just want to get home.

For me, there was less fear in the beginning. I became more fearful as time went on—more fearful as I witnessed scenes like the exploding Messerschmitt. The further we went into Russia, the more dangerous it was and the more fear we felt. I wouldn't have wanted to be a Messerschmitt pilot there. They were asked to do what no one should be asked to do. The odds against them were overwhelming, and that's why so many did not come back."

Wilhelm Stoll, gunner in a *Stukageschwader.* After the war, he met Adolf Galland and asked him about combat in Bf 109s. Galland replied simply: "You're a hunter in a Messerschmitt." *Wilhelm Stoll*

ADVANCED VERSIONS

Bf 109E-5 through 109K and Special-Use Aircraft

Suggestions from veterans of the blitzkriegs and Battle of Britain, along with engineering innovations, brought continuous advancements to the basic Bf 109 airframe during the first half of World War II. Through these incremental changes, the Bf 109 not only kept pace, but alternately leapfrogged its arch-rival, the Supermarine Spitfire. The Bf 109 was still among the top fighters in the world as Hitler turned his attention eastward for the conquest of Russia.

The Bf 109's horsepower was equal to or better than opposing fighters, and the Bosch fuel injection had given it the edge in many dogfights over Great Britain and the Channel. Its performance at high altitude was superb. Its armament was heavier than many contemporaries. Its short range had proven a debilitating handicap, but that was soon easily overcome with better drop tanks. A large percentage of losses stemmed from mismanagement on the strategic level, as the *Jagdgeschwadern* were ordered to tempt fate daily by flying to the absolute limits of range during the Battle of Britain.

Werner Mölder's personal Bf 109E-4, with eagle emblem on the nose. The same eagle would appear on his Bf 109F flown in Russia. Mölders preferred the lighter armament of the E-4 (without the MG FF nose cannon of the E-3). He advocated skill of marksmanship and increased maneuverability that came with lighter weight. Later, he would favor reduction to one 20mm cannon and two 7.9mm machine guns for the F series—a point hotly debated by Galland, who considered any reduction in weapons a step backward. *Bowers Collection*

The Bf 109 is a remarkable story of longevity, being designed in 1934 and remaining a front-line fighter through the war's end in 1945, but the design showed its age as the war reached midpoint. Great Britain and Russia made strides in aeronautical design, and the United States plunged into the fray with its great resources and newer, faster, and ever more deadly aircraft.

The Bf 109 would stay competitive through the succession of Emils after the E-3 and E-4 of Battle of Britain fame. It would leapfrog once again with the Friedrich series, which many agree marked the apex of the Bf 109's design. This was the most dramatic advancement yet. The most pronounced visual changes came with the Friedrich. Gone were the sharp, angular lines, now replaced by a rounded, sleeker shape—a rounding of the square wingtips, an aerodynamically cleaner cowl, and a propeller spinner lending a bullet-like shape to the nose. Next in the succession, the Gustavs were the most heavily armed, in order to meet the increasing threat of USAAF and RAF bombers. The K series was the most powerful. But at its most powerful and potent, the Bf 109 had traded off too much for speed and firepower, and lapsed into decline while the Allied fighters remained hard-hitting and maneuverable.

Instead of being the leader, innovator, and standard-setter, it became the underdog in a constant game of catch-up. And, strange as it sounds, it was at this last stage that the Bf 109 was built in its greatest numbers.

Bf 109E-4/N

Knowing that increasingly formidable fighter opponents awaited them in Great Britain, German engineers looked for ways to improve the odds in their favor. Content with the airframe of the E-4, they decided an increase in engine power was the answer. Thus, the E-4/N was powered by a high-performance Daimler-Benz powerplant variant, the 1,200-horsepower DB 601N with an 8.2 compression ratio that required the higher 100-octane fuel (versus a 6.9 compression ratio for the DB 601A that used 87 octane).

Along with the 1,200-horsepower, high-compression DB 601N engine came:

A loose *Schwarm* of Bf 109E-4/Trops fly above the Mediterranean. They carry 300-liter belly gas tanks that enable them to make the hop from Italy to North Africa. The belly tank extended range by about 170 miles. This metal tank was a vast improvement over earlier Luftwaffe external tanks, which were made of molded plywood and leaked badly. *Ethell Collection*

- Improved fuel injection.
- An automatically controlled hydraulic coupling on the supercharger drive.
- Flat piston heads instead of concave.

The E-4/N also was fitted with bomb racks to allow the option of the *Jabo* role. Like previous 4Bs, it could carry either one 250-kilogram (552.5-pound) or four 50-kilogram (110.5-pound) bombs.

Bf 109E-5 and E-6 (Reconnaissance)

Two short-range reconnaissance variants were adapted from the E-4 design. The Bf 109E-5 was essentially the same as the E-4, but with wing cannons removed and an Rb 21/18 camera fitted within the fuselage, just aft of the wings, pointing directly downward.

The E-6 was the twin of the E-4/N, powered by the same high-performance Daimler-Benz DB 601N with 1,200 horsepower and needing higher octane fuel. But in its reconnaissance role, it had no bomb rack. Unlike the E-5, it usually had wing-mounted cannons, and the camera was a different model, the Rb 50/30.

Bf 109E-4/N Specifications

Dimensions—Wingspan: 32 feet, 4 1/2 inches. Length: 28 feet, 8 inches.

Weight—Empty: 4,445 pounds. Gross: 6,180 pounds (when loaded as *Jabo*).

Powerplant—Daimler-Benz DB 601N inverted V-12, liquid-cooled engine. Takeoff horsepower: 1,200.

Armament—Two 7.9mm MG 17 machine guns (capacity of 500 rounds per gun), mounted above the engine in the cowl. Two wing-mounted MG FF cannons. And optionally, one 250-kilogram (552.5-pound) or four 50-kilogram (110.5-pound) bombs.

Performance—Maximum speed: 373 miles per hour at 19,700 feet. Ceiling: 32,800 feet.

Bf 109E-5 and E-6 Specifications

Dimensions—Wingspan: 32 feet, 4 1/2 inches. Length: 28 feet, 8 inches.

Weight—Empty: 4,415 pounds. Gross: 5,190 pounds.

Powerplant—E-5: Daimler-Benz DB 601Aa inverted V-12, liquid-cooled engine. Takeoff horsepower: 1,100. E-6: Daimler-Benz DB 601N inverted V-12, liquid-cooled engine. Takeoff horsepower: 1,200.

Armament—Two 7.9mm MG 17 machine guns, mounted above the engine in the cowl. E-6: This armament, usually along with two wing-mounted MG FF cannons.

Maximum Speed—E-5: 357 miles per hour at 19,700 feet. E-6: 373 miles per hour at 19,700 feet.

Transition begins from Emils to Friedrichs in first-line *Jagdgeschwadern*. Here we see two new Bf 109Fs in line with some of the hundreds of Emils soon to be phased out of combat units. The large, dome-like spinner is the most readily recognizable difference, but the Friedrich was actually all new from the firewall forward: the cowl and underside are rounder and more streamlined. *Bowers Collection*

Bf 109E-7, E-7/Z, and E-7/U2

The E-7 began reaching *Jagdgeschwadern* in late summer 1940. It was virtually the same as the E-4/N, with the same DB 601N powerplant and armament, but addressed the great shortcomings in range by using jettisonable fuel tanks. The E-7's differences were:

- Fittings underneath allowing for the option of either a 250-kilogram (552.5-pound) bomb load or a 300-liter drop tank.
- The spinner (on most) tipped by a rounded point instead of a barrel opening for an engine-mounted cannon.

The E-7/U2 experimented with 5mm armor bolted under the radiator, cooler, and fuel pump, all of which had been found highly vulnerable to ground fire as well as fighter fire underneath. Armor was particularly critical in North Africa, where ground support was the primary role.

The E-7/Z experimented with a nitrous oxide power-boosting system (GM-1) in hopes of improving performance at high altitude. Both U and Z enjoyed some degree of success and these features saw use in a number of later versions of the Bf 109.

Bf 109E-7 Specifications

Dimensions—Wingspan: 32 feet, 4 1/2 inches. Length: 28 feet, 8 inches.

Weight—Empty: 4,440 pounds. Gross: 5,520 pounds.

Powerplant—Daimler-Benz DB 601N inverted V-12, liquid-cooled engine. Takeoff horsepower: 1,200.

Armament—Two 7.9mm MG 17 machine guns, mounted above the engine in the cowl and two wing-mounted MG FF cannons.

Performance—Maximum speed: 366 miles per hour at 19,700 feet. Ceiling: 36,000 feet.

Bf 109E-8 and E-9

In quick succession following the E-7 were the E-8 and E-9 in late fall 1940. The airframe remained unchanged, but both new versions had a new, more powerful, Daimler-Benz powerplant, the DB 601E, which would see service in many Bf 109 versions to come. The E-8 had the same armament as the E-7.

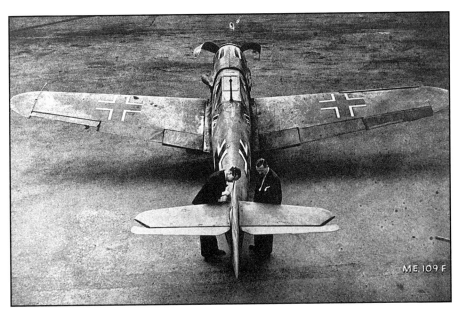

This Bf 109F has bellied-in nearly intact. It has been raised back on its landing gear and will be restored for testing. Here, British engineers pay special attention to the Bf 109's new and unfamiliar cantilevered tailplane that is unlike the braced tailplane of previously captured Emils. They no doubt also paused curiously at the new, round-tip wings that replace the signature square wing tips of all previous Bf 109 versions. *Kalamazoo Air Zoo*

The last of the Emils, the E-9, was an E-8 minus wing cannons and equipped for photo reconnaissance, with either an Rb 50/30 or two Rb 32/7 cameras mounted inside the fuselage just aft of the wings and pointing directly downward.

Flight and combat-related advancements included:
- Daimler-Benz DB 601E with 1,300 horsepower.
- Increased maximum revolutions per minute (inherent to the DB 601E) and improved supercharger.
- Back armor added to protect the pilot.

Bf 109E-4/Trop and E-5/Trop

First arriving in North Africa on April 21, 1941, both E-4/Trop and E-5/Trop versions saw action immediately with 1/JG 27. All had been built as standard E-4s and E-5s, then tropicalized en route while in Sicily. Tropicalization included:

- Fitting a dust filter over the supercharger air intake.
- Emergency desert survival equipment, including a carbine.

Bf 109T

Already in the 1930s, the forward-looking German Navy had ambitious plans to add aircraft carriers to its fleet. Keels had been laid for the carriers *Graf Zeppelin* and *Peter Strasser*, and the *Traegergruppe* (carrier group) was being organized with dive bombers and escort fighters in mind. Fulfilling the need for the ship's complement of fighters would be the Bf 109T, *T* standing for *Traeger*, and Junkers' carrier-based version of its Ju 87.

The Gerhard Fieseler Werke had been given the charge of converting 10 Bf 109E-1s then on the assembly line to *Trager* class aircraft. After conversion, the new, somewhat ungainly looking Bf 109T had:
- Wings increased in span and hinged for manual folding.
- Spoilers on the upper surface of the wings (steepening angle of approach for a short landing distance).

Bf 109E-8 and E-9 Specifications

Dimensions—Wingspan: 32 feet, 4 1/2 inches. Length: 28 feet, 8 inches.

Weight—E-8: Empty: 4,460 pounds. Gross: 5,560 pounds. E-9: Empty: 4,415 pounds. Gross: 5,300 pounds.

Powerplant—Daimler-Benz DB 601E inverted V-12, liquid-cooled engine. Takeoff horsepower: 1,300.

Armament—E-8: Two 7.9mm MG 17 machine guns, mounted above the engine in the cowl, two wing-mounted MG FF cannons, and one 250-kilogram (552.5-pound) or four 50-kilogram (110.5-pound) bombs. E-9: Two cowl-mounted machine guns only.

Performance—E-8: Maximum speed: 366 miles per hour at 19,700 feet. E-9: Maximum speed: 378 miles per hour. Ceiling: 32,800 feet.

Bf 109T-2 Specifications

Dimensions—Wingspan: 36 feet, 2 1/2 inches. Length: 28 feet, 8 inches. Height: 8 feet, 6 inches.

Weight—Empty: 4,905 pounds. Gross maximum: 6,786 pounds.

Powerplant—Daimler-Benz DB 601N supercharged, inverted V-12, liquid-cooled engine. Takeoff horsepower: 1,200.

Armament—Two 7.9mm MG 17 machine guns mounted above the engine in the cowl, two wing-mounted MG FF cannons, and one 250-kilogram (552.5-pound) or four 50-kilogram (110.5-pound) bombs.

Performance—Maximum speed: 357 miles per hour at 19,700 feet. Ceiling: 34,500 feet.

Me 109F
DAIMLER-BENZ DB-601E

The British Air Ministry's rendering of the new Bf 109F. The drawing was borrowed for the USAAF's Aircraft Evaluation Report No. 110, dated July 2, 1943. *National Archives*

It had a refined aerodynamic shape that better matched the increased power of the Daimler-Benz DB 601E powerplant. Only the fuselage between the firewall and the tail remained the same. The wings, tailplane, cowl, and airscrew were all new.

The redesigned wing retained its spar structure, but improved lift and reduced drag. The Friedrich:

- Reduced drag by recessing the under-wing radiators further up into the wings, flattening the air intake.
- Had a thinner high-speed airfoil.
- Rounded off the "signature 109" square wingtips into semielliptical wingtips.
- Reduced wing area by about 1 square foot because of modified plan-form.
- Changed the slotted ailerons to the standard Frise-type surfaces, and shortened their span.
- Changed the slotted flaps to the close-fitting standard type and reduced their size and area (and removed a linkage connecting ailerons and flaps in preceding versions).

The automatic slats remained, but armament internal to the new, slender wing was out of the question.

Other refinements common to the series included:

- Improved armament—a single, faster-firing, engine-mounted cannon, the Mauser MG 151 (replacing the pair of wing-mounted 20mm MG FF cannons).
- A cleaner, symmetrical cowl that improved aerodynamics.
- Wider propeller blades that were shorter by 2 inches, improving the constant-speed airscrew.
- Larger, bullet-shaped airscrew spinner.
- A supercharger air intake that extended further away from the cowl to increase ram-air flow.
- A deeper oil cooler bath on the under the chin.
- A partially retractable tail-wheel.
- Greater slant of mainwheel legs.
- A reshaped rudder, reduced in area from 8.1 to 7.5 square feet.
- A cantilevered tailplane that eliminated the need for struts to brace the horizontal tailplane.

- Stronger structure and landing gear to compensate for the extra stresses of carrier landings.
- An arrester hook attached just aft of the seventh fuselage frame.
- A catapult spool attached between the fifth and sixth fuselage frames.
- Locking tailwheels.

The construction of 70 Ts was undertaken by Fieseler, but before any could fly there was a sudden change of strategic direction that suspended work temporarily on the German carriers in October 1939, then halted it altogether in May 1940. The order for these 70 aircraft took a peculiar turn: Only seven were to be completed to full *Traeger* specifications. These were designated Bf 109T-1. The remaining 63 were to be built as land-based fighters with all *Traeger* modifications deleted, except for the increased wingspan. Designated Bf 109T-2, these were without arrester hook, catapult spool, etc. Those eventually saw service with I/JG 77 in Norway as fighter-bombers on short airstrips.

Bf 109F (Friedrich)

The Friedrich series began production in late 1940 and superseded the large Emil air fleet throughout 1941. In the continuing one-upmanship with the British, the F-1 would prove itself superior against the Spitfire (until the Mk. V leapfrogged once again).

To some, the Friedrich is the definitive Bf 109—the "crest of its evolution." It was the purest form of the aircraft, before the changing nature of the air war placed demands on the design that deteriorated handling and lift. It was considered by many pilots to be the best to fly.

Bf 109F-1

As it turned out, the new Mauser MG 151 engine-mounted cannon was not yet available, so F-1s used a single MG FF firing through the spinner. And the DB 601E engine was not yet available in large numbers, so the DB 601N was installed.

In February 1941, a series of mysterious crashes caused the first batch of F-1s to be grounded. Based on the pilot description of severe vibration (the last words radioed

Fast and agile, the Friedrich made an excellent reconnaissance platform. This F-6 is essentially an F-4 with two MG 17 machine guns in the cowl, but no engine-mounted cannon, nor *panzerglas* in front, all to shave off weight and squeeze out more speed and range. Since range was needed for long-distance intelligence gathering, F-6s usually carried a 300-liter belly tank. Here, a camera body is lifted into the cockpit for positioning behind the pilot's seat, where a high-magnification lens is already installed. The lens, either wide-angle or long-lens to zero in on specific targets, points directly downward through a special plate with a hole for the lens, fitted on the underside just aft of the cockpit. Even after Gustavs became the standard fighter and the G-8 reconnaissance fighter entered service, F-6s remained in use because of their speed and agility over similarly equipped Gustav reconnaissance aircraft. *Bowers Collection*

by two pilots killed in the crashes), engineers suspected the engine. But tests of the engine showed no problems; plus there had been no such vibration with the DB 601N in the Bf 109E-4/N. F-1s were allowed to fly again, but soon there was another crash in which the aircraft lost its tail.

The external tail bracing, common to all previous Bf 109 versions, finally had been discarded and a cantilevered tailplane took its place. Therein lay the problem: Vibration had caused rivets to pop, leading to structural failure. Rather than simply adding the struts back on, engineers chose to attach external stiffening plates along the fuselage sides. The problem was resolved for the interim and marked for fixing with the next version.

Armament modification drew more than a little criticism. The late Emils' firepower of two MG 17 cowl-mounted guns and two wing-mounted cannons was reduced in the Friedrich to two MG 17 cowl-mounted guns and a single engine-mounted cannon. Werner Mölders welcomed the change, citing improved maneuverability and the advantage of firepower aimed right along the pilot's axis. Walter Oesau and Adolf Galland both criticized the change, saying it was a "retrogressive step." Oesau

Bf 109F-1 and F-2 Specifications

Dimensions—Wingspan: 32 feet, 6 1/2 inches. Length: 29 feet, 8 inches. Height: 8 feet, 6 1/3 inches.

Weight—Empty: 4,440 pounds. Gross: 5,760 pounds (F-1) and 5,960 pounds (F-2).

Powerplant—Daimler-Benz DB 601N inverted V-12, liquid-cooled engine. Takeoff horsepower: 1,200.

Armament—F-1: One engine-mounted MG FF cannon and two 7.9mm MG 17 machine guns, mounted above the engine in the cowl. F-2: One engine-mounted 15mm MG 151 cannon and two 7.9mm MG 17 machine guns, mounted above the engine in the cowl.

Performance—Maximum speed: 369 (F-1) miles per hour and 366 mils per hour (F-2) at 19,700 feet.

continued to fly his favorite old E-4 until lack of spare parts forced him to accept the F-series fighters.

Bf 109F-2

In April 1941, the F-2 began reaching front-line *Jagdgeschwadern* in the west on the Channel Front—JG 2, 26, 27, and 53 (many eastern units preparing for Operation *Barbarossa* would receive them later, in time for the invasion of Russia). The intended cannon armament for the Friedrichs became available, but the intended engine (DB 601E) still was unavailable. So, in summary, changes to the F-2 included:

- The faster firing, engine-mounted 15mm MG 151 cannon (although not the 20mm MG 151 originally specified).
- Local internal strengthening in the tail that eliminated the need for external stiffeners (except for the very first F-2s off the line).
- Round wheel wells for mainwheels (versus square-end wheel wells that anticipated wheel-well covers that never materialized).

Bf 109F-3

The F-3 was the same as the F-2, except for powerplant. The DB 601E finally was available by the beginning of 1942. The new engine used 87-octane fuel instead of 96-octane, so the octane triangle on the fuselage aft of the cockpit noted 87 instead of "C3." The F-3 had a short production run, equipping some of the Channel units.

Bf 109F-4

The F-4 finally was bedecked with the specifications intended for the F-series. As such, it was considered by many to be the "best of the best"—the best version in the best series of the Bf 109. It had the DB 601E engine (as did

The stablemate of the Bf 109: The venerable Focke-Wulf Fw 190. As soon as the Fw 190 entered combat in summer 1941, it was immediately apparent that the new fighter could outperform the Bf 109's arch rival, the Spitfire, and other fighters in the Allied inventory at the time. With a 1,700-horsepower 18-cylinder BMW radial engine, the aircraft had a maximum speed of 408 miles per hour. It had some performance problems at first, especially at higher altitudes, but these were overcome, and the aircraft remained superior to Allied fighters through 1943. *National Archives*

its immediate predecessor) and the improved cannon, the 20mm MG 151. With the larger shell, ammunition capacity was reduced from 200 to 150 rounds. The F-4 was everything the Friedrich was intended from the beginning. A few other miscellaneous improvements accompanied the version:

- Better self-sealing fuel tank.
- Improved *panzerglas* windscreen.
- Protection behind and angling over the pilot: *panzerglas* framed by armor plate (for neck, shoulders, and the back of the head).
- Triggering mechanisms allowed the cannon and machine guns to be fired separately or simultaneously.
- A larger, more bulbous supercharger intake.

The F-4 was produced in the largest number of the Friedrich series.

Bf 109F-3 and F-4 Specifications

Dimensions—Wingspan: 32 feet, 6 1/2 inches. Length: 29 feet, 8 inches. Height: 8 feet, 6 1/3 inches.

Weight—Empty: 4,330 pounds. Gross: 6,200 pounds (F-3) and 6,220 pounds (F-4).

Powerplant—Daimler-Benz DB 601E inverted V-12, liquid-cooled engine. Takeoff horsepower: 1,300.

Armament—F-3: One engine-mounted 15mm MG 151 cannon and two 7.9mm MG 17 machine guns, mounted above the engine in the cowl. F-4: The same except the cannon—one 20mm MG 151.

Performance—Maximum speed: 388 miles per hour at 21,325 feet. Maximum range: 355 miles. Ceiling: 39,400 feet.

Bf 109F-5 and F-6 (Reconnaissance)

Like the fifth and sixth versions from the E-series, the fifth and sixth versions of the F-series were adapted into short-range reconnaissance versions. The Bf 109F-5 was essentially the same as the F-4, but the engine-mounted cannon was removed and a camera fitted within the fuselage, just aft of the wings, pointing directly downward. The F-6 improved on that by removing *all* armament—both engine-mounted and cowl-mounted guns—to increase speed and range, and providing a special camera bay that could accommodate a variety of cameras: Rb 20/30, Rb 50/30, or Rb 75/30. Both were fitted for fuselage racks allowing a 300-liter drop tank to extend range further.

Bf 109F-5 and F-6 Specifications

Dimensions—Wingspan: 32 feet, 6 1/2 inches. Length: 29 feet, 8 inches. Height: 8 feet, 6 1/4 inches.

Weight—Gross: 6,545 pounds (F-5) and 6,425 pounds (F-6).

Powerplant—Daimler-Benz DB 601E inverted V-12, liquid-cooled engine. Takeoff horsepower: 1,300.

Armament—F-5: Two 7.9mm MG 17 machine guns, mounted above the engine in the cowl F-6: None.

Performance—Maximum speed: 373 miles per hour at 19,700 feet. Maximum range: 622 miles (F-5) and 684 miles (F-6). Ceiling: 39,400 feet.

F-Series Variants

Jabo versions of the Friedrich differed only in the equipment needed for bomb carrying and release. For both the Bf 109F-1/B and F-4/B, there were bomb-fusing battery boxes inside the fuselage and ventral bomb carriers. Both fighter-bombers carried a single 250-kilogram (552.5-pound) bomb. The F-4 had the greatest numbers in both fighter and fighter-bomber versions. In 1941, these were used extensively by JG 2 and 26 *Jabo Staffeln*, with great effect, including the sinking of many Royal Navy ships by 10 (*Jabo*)/JG 26.

The F-1 saw service in North Africa, which required tropicalization. However, the first production tropicalized aircraft were F-2s (previous versions had been retrofitted).

Like the Bf 109E-7/Z, one Friedrich version—the F-2—experimented with the GM-1 nitrous oxide boost system. To further benefit high-altitude flight, a wider-bladed VDM propeller and a larger supercharger intake was installed. Some versions in the Bf 109G series would have these modifications as standard.

Bf 109G (Gustav)

Pilots realized how tight the race was for superiority in aircraft design and how advancements gave only slight, fleeting advantage. The leapfrogging of the Bf 109 and Spitfire over one another came to be expected during the years 1940 through 1942. The first Gustavs came off the assembly line during summer 1942. After flying a succession of fighters, Heinz Knoke knew the routine and noted in his log for October 2, 1942: "The Messerschmitt 109E was replaced several months ago by the improved 109F. A few days ago the first models of the 'G' type started coming off the assembly lines. The performance of the 'Gustav' (as we call the Messerschmitt 109G) seems, for the time being at least, to be definitely superior to that of the Spitfire."

The first Gustavs looked like Friedrichs, but had the more powerful DB 605A. They were sleek and fast, but with later Gustavs, the age and limitations of the Bf 109 design began to show.

More modern designs had come to the Luftwaffe the year before, when the Focke-Wulf Fw 190A had come into being. Even in the Gustav series, the most powerful yet, the Bf 109 could not carry the armament of the Fw 190, with its four cannons and two machine guns. The Fw 190 had a sturdier airframe and proved more maneuverable at low to medium altitudes. So some engineers concluded that the Bf 109 should be phased out and replaced with the new design. Many loyal combat pilots chose to differ. But beyond personal sentiment, there were practical reasons why the Bf 109's operational life did not end at this point—not the least of which was the fact that the Fw 190's performance deteriorated badly at altitudes over 20,000 feet. The Fw 190's prowess at low and medium altitudes was well known, but combat was not limited to those altitudes–in a defensive role against high-flying Allied bombers, combat was happening more and more at altitudes of 20,000 to 26,000 feet. Plus, Germany continued Bf 109 production because the relentless day-and-night Allied bombing campaign gave no time for interlude to stop factories and tool up for a new, modern design of aircraft. As a stopgap measure, they pulled together all the armament and equipment needed into the tiny Bf 109 airframe and called it Gustav.

At this stage of the war, defense against Allied bombers became the ultimate objective. It took more than two rifle-caliber cowl machine gun and single cannon to shoot down the rugged bombers. To meet that need, three things were necessary: altitude, speed, and firepower. *Anything* else was secondary. The Gustav sought the best balance of the three, and the biggest tradeoff was maneuverability. This didn't make the Bf 109G a sitting duck for the Mustang and other highly capable enemy fighters, but it was a severe handicap.

The DB 605 increased horsepower by more than 13 percent over its predecessor, the DB 601E, but it also increased weight. The outside dimensions of the engine did not increase, and thus did not require alterations to the airframe, but the increased weight begat a sturdier frame. A sturdier frame further added weight, which begat sturdier landing gear. Sturdier landing gear added more weight, which begat increased wing loading. This resulted in a heavy, unforgiving airplane with poor handling characteristics like a wider turning radius and worsened stall behavior. This was an entirely different aircraft from the one in which Dr. Wurster powered through 23 counterclockwise and 21 clockwise turns over Travemünde.

Also in support of the new higher altitude combat was the implementation of pressurized cabins. Several Gustav versions had pressurized cabins, but far more of the nonpressurized were manufactured.

Beyond the new DB 605 engine, other modifications common to the series were:

The DB 605A of *Black 9* is hoisted out of the airframe for an overhaul. The Gustav's DB 605A powerplant superseded the DB 601 (in its A, Aa, N, and E versions) used in the Emil and Friedrich versions. The new engine increased compression ratio substantially. The DB 601A's ratio was 6.9 to 1; the DB 605A's ratio was to 7.5 to 1 in the starboard cylinder bank and 7.3 to 1 in the port. The increased ratio was accomplished without increased outside engine dimensions. Dry engine weight increased from the DB 601A's 1,366 pounds to more than 1,500 pounds for the DB 605A. Note the aircraft's steel machined main-wheels that were used in later Gustavs (less expensive than the spoked cast main-wheels of earlier versions). This photo is dated May 5, 1944. *Ethell Collection*

Der Buele (the bump): Showing the swellings of overdesign, the Bf 109's tiny airframe ran out of room inside and so had to bulge outward. The bumps in front of the windshield accommodate the breeches of the 13mm MG 131 machine guns equipping later Gustavs. The half-moon bumps on the wings accommodate the larger mainwheels when retracted. The underwing swellings are gondolas that house the 20mm MG 151 cannons. *Bowers Collection*

- The wider-bladed propeller, introduced with the F-2/Z.
- Standardization of the wider propeller tested with the Bf 109F-2/Z.
- Two small air scoops on the cowl (to overcome a rash of oil leaks onto the hot engine during overheating, which erupted in fire) to cool the oil reservoir.[13]
- Wheelwells for the main landing gear in the square-top shape of earlier versions (the plan was to equip the version with covers that fully concealed the wheels, but this did not happen).
- A new fuel tank design.
- Alteration of cockpit glass that eliminated the small triangular window on the two oblique panels to the left and right of the windscreen.

More than 10,000 Gustavs were produced in the 10 main combat versions of the series—the most of any. The G-6 was produced in the largest number of the Gustav series.

Bf 109G-1 (pressurized cabin) and G-2 (nonpressurized)

In late May 1942, the first G-1s were introduced to *Jagdgeschwadern* stationed in the west, as the first-line defense against the Allied bombers from England. (The G-2, built side-by-side on the production line, actually reached operational units several weeks earlier.) The most important change introduced with the G-1 was a pressurized cabin.

Cabin pressurization enabled the Bf 109 to match the altitude of high-flying bombers; special high-altitude *Staffeln* were formed within JG 2 and later JG 26 for this

purpose. These aircraft were specially modified by removing armor, fitting a GM 1 (nitrous oxide) power-booster, and mounting a 300-liter drop tank.

Beyond the DB 605A engine, flight-related advancements of the G-1 included:

- "Cold wall" pressurized cabin, with rubber seals at joints.
- Heavier canopy, modified for pressurization.
- Fittings to carry two 300-liter drop tanks at strong points on the wings, just inboard of the leading-edge slots.

The G-2 was virtually identical to the G-1, but without a pressurized cabin. The nonpressurized G-2 had a pair of tiny air scoops mounted just beneath the canopy's small oblique windows, just to the left and right of the tiny windscreen.

The G-1 was tropicalized for use in dusty desert conditions, as earlier Emils and Friedrichs had been. Beyond the normal tropicalization—air filter and desert survival kit—there was retrofitting of armament. The two cowl-mounted 7.9mm MG 17 machine guns were replaced by two 13-mm MG 131 machine guns. (See G-6.) The new supercharger intake, round instead of square, required a new dust filter. After so-so performance from a German filter, an Italian-designed filter was adopted for use in North Africa, the Balkans, Southern Russia, or anywhere dust was a problem.

Both the G-2 and G-4 could be adapted as a fast reconnaissance aircraft under the designation G-2/R-2 and

Laden with both a 500-kilogram (1,102-pound) bomb and external wing tanks, the Bf 109G-2/R is prepared for its role as a long-range light bomber. It was a role the Bf 109 could not gracefully accept. The cumbrous fighter was ripe for the picking if bounced en route to target. Even without bombs and external fuel tanks, the Gustav's weight diminished much of the dogfighting capability that made the Bf 109 legendary. This one has been further weighed down with an auxiliary tail-wheel that provided clearance for the underslung peripherals. *Bowers Collection*

A 21-centimeter (8.2-inch) rocket tube is another underwing attachment. With a tube under each wing, this G-6/R2 had an infantry-support role. It is rarely seen photographed, primarily because it did not have extensive use. *Bowers Collectio*

Bf 109G-1 and G-2 Specifications

Dimensions—Wingspan: 32 feet, 6 1/2 inches. Length: 29 feet, 8 inches. Height: 8 feet, 2 1/2 inches.

Weight—Empty: 4,968 pounds. Gross: 7,055 pounds.

Powerplant—Daimler-Benz DB 605A inverted V-12, liquid-cooled engine. Takeoff horsepower: 1,475.

Armament—G-1: One engine-mounted 20mm MG 151 cannon and two MG 17 machine guns, mounted above the engine in the cowl. G-2: Four MG 17 machine guns, two cowl-mounted, two wing-mounted.

Performance—Maximum speed: 398 miles per hour at 20,670 feet. Maximum range: 348 miles. Ceiling: 39,700 feet.

G-4/R-2. For greater speed and maneuverability, neither retained the MG 151 cannon or GM 1 system; much like in Friedrich reconnaissance versions, an Rb 50/30 camera was installed within the fuselage just aft of the wings. Both usually carried a 300-liter drop tank.

Bf 109G-3 (pressurized cabin) and G-4 (nonpressurized)

The G-3 and G-4 were also produced simultaneously, and flew off to operational units at the same time (unlike the G-1 and G-2). The G-3 and G-4 differed in cabin pressurization and armament: The G-3 had two cowl-mounted MG 17 machine guns and engine-mounted 20mm MG 151; the G-4 did not have the engine-mounted MG 151, but a G-4 variant would be the first to increase firepower dramatically. Some pilots had criticized the Bf 109's armament since the introduction of the Friedrich. They leveled more pointed criticism at the Gustav, reminding designers of its primary purpose:

To defend the Reich against the RAF and USAAF heavy bombers, now coming around the clock. To overcome "lack of punch," the G-4/R-6 was fitted with 20mm MG 151 cannons mounted in underwing gondolas. This was called *Rüstsatz* 6 armament, installed in kit form in the field.

Since the G series' weight increased severely with the new engine, armament, and other equipment, landing gear was modified. To help in ground handling, particularly in landing the heavier aircraft, G-3s were given larger mainwheels. To make room for the larger wheels, the wings were modified with a bulge on the upper surface. The tailwheel was retractable but was usually locked down, so a rubber boot was fitted.

Refinements of the G-3 and G-4 included:
- The FuG 16 radio, which replaced the FuG 7a. This required small changes to the rigging of the antenna wire.
- Larger main-wheels (650x150mm replaced by 660x160mm) and larger tailwheel (290x110mm replaced by 350x135mm).

G-5 (pressurized cabin) and G-6 (nonpressurized)

The G-5 answered the call for greater armament needed to pummel the Allied bombers out of the sky and to match the harder hitting Fw 190. The cowl-mounted 7.9mm MG 17 machine guns, installed on Bf 109s since almost the beginning, were replaced with 13mm MG 131 machine guns. The weapons change caused these versions to be nicknamed *der Buele* (the bump), because the larger machine guns' breeches and ammunition feeders required a bump on each side of the nose, just in front of the cockpit. Consequently, the machine gun troughs in the cowl were moved slightly rearward.

As the Bf 109 continued to suffer ground looping, sudden tail darting, and collapsing landing gear throughout the war, engineers tried one obvious solution: tricycle landing gear. Tricycle gear had certain advantages, especially for the many inexperienced pilots filling out the ranks of the *Jagdgeschwadern* later in the war. The aircraft, designated Bf 309A-1, never reached production. The project model carried two MG 131s and one Mk 108, the same as some Gustav versions. *Bowers Collection*

Bf 109G-14

1. Starboard navigation light
2. Starboard wingtip
3. Fixed trim tab
4. Starboard Frise-type aileron
5. Flush-riveted stressed wing skin
6. Handley-Page automatic leading-edge slot
7. Slot control linkage
8. Slot equalizer rod
9. Aileron control linkage
10. Fabric-covered flap section
11. Wheel fairing
12. Port fuselage
13. Machine-gun ammunition feed fairing
14. Port 13-mm Rheinmetall-Borsig MG 131 machine gun
15. Engine accessories
16. Daimler-Benz DB 605AM 12-cylinder inverted-Vee
      liquid-cooled engine
17. Detachable cowling panel
18. Oil filter access
19. Oil tank
20. Propeller pitch-change mechanism
21. VDM electrically operated
      constant-speed propeller
22. Spinner
23. Engine-mounted cannon muzzle
24. Blast tube
25. Propeller hub
26. Spinner back plate
27. Auxiliary cooling intakes
28. Coolant header tank
29. Anti-vibration rubber engine
      mounting pads
30. Electron-forged engine bearer
31. Engine bearer support
      strut attachment
32. Plug leads
33. Exhaust manifold
      fairing strip
34. Ejector exhausts
35. Cowling fasteners
36. Oil cooler
37. Oil cooler intake
38. Starboard mainwheel
39. Oil cooler outlet flap
40. Wing root fillet
41. Wing/fuselage fairing
42. Firewall/bulkhead
43. Supercharger air intake
44. Supercharger assembly
45. 20-mm cannon magazine drum
46. 13-mm machine-gun ammunition feed
47. Engine bearer upper attachment
48. Ammunition feed fairing
49. 13-mm Rheinmetall-Borsig MG 131 machine-gun breeches
50. Instrument panel
51. 20-mm Mauser MG 151/20 cannon breech
52. Heel rests
53. Rudder pedals
54. Undercarriage emergency retraction cables
55. Fuselage frame
56. Wing/fuselage fairing
57. Undercarriage emergency retraction handwheel (outboard)
58. Tail trim handwheel (inboard)
59. Seat harness
60. Throttle lever
61. Control column

62. Cockpit ventilation inlet
63. Revi 16B reflector gunsight (folding)
64. Armored windshield frame
65. Anti-glare gunsight screen
66. 3-1/2 inch (90-mm) Panzerglas windscreen
67. Erla Haube clear-vision hinged canopy
68. Galland Panzerglas head/back panel
69. Canopy contoured frame
70. Canopy hinges (starboard)
71. Canopy release catch
72. Pilot's bucket-type seat
      (0.3-inch/8-mm back armor)
73. Under floor contoured fuel
      tank (88 Imperial gallons/
      400 liters of 87 octane B4)
74. Fuselage frame

75. Circular access panel
76. Tail trimming cable conduit
77. Wireless leads
78. MW-50 (methanol/water)
      tank capacity: 25 Imperial
      gallons/114 liters)
79. Handhold
80. Fuselage decking
81. Aerial mast
82. DF loop
83. Oxygen cylinders (three)
84. Filler pipe
85. FuG wireless equipment packs
      (16ZY communications and 25 IFF)
86. Main fuel filler cap
87. Aerial
88. Fuselage top keel (connector stringer)
89. Aerial lead-in
90. Fuselage skin-plating sections
91. "U" stringers

92. Fuselage frames (monocoque construction)
93. Tail trimming cables
94. Tail fin root fairing
95. Starboard fixed tailplane
96. Elevator balance
97. Starboard elevator
98. Geared elevator tab
99. All-wood tail fin construction
100. Aerial attachment
101. Rudder upper hinge bracket
102. Rudder post
103. Fabric-covered wooden rudder structure
104. Geared rudder tab
105. Rear navigation light
106. Port elevator
107. Elevator geared tab

125. Ventral IFF Aerial
126. Master compass
127. Elevator control linkage
128. Wing root fillet
129. Camber changing flap
130. Ducted coolant radiator
131. Wing stringers
132. Wing rear pick-up point
133. Spar/fuselage upper pin joint (horizontal)
134. Spar/fuselage lower pin joint (vertical)
135. Flap equalizer rod
136. Rüstsatz-3 auxiliary fuel tank ventral rack

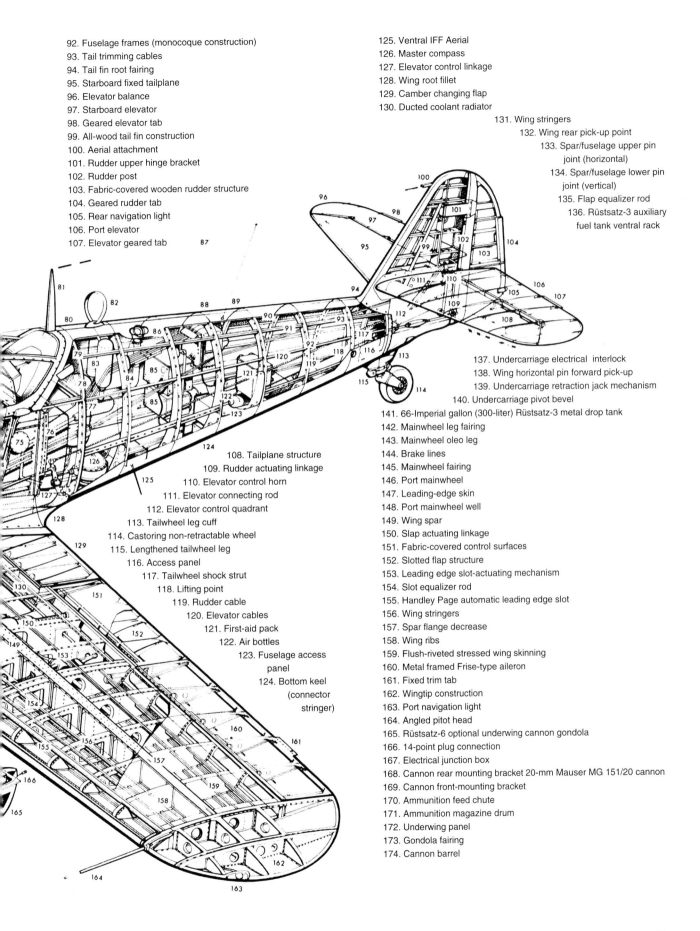

108. Tailplane structure
109. Rudder actuating linkage
110. Elevator control horn
111. Elevator connecting rod
112. Elevator control quadrant
113. Tailwheel leg cuff
114. Castoring non-retractable wheel
115. Lengthened tailwheel leg
116. Access panel
117. Tailwheel shock strut
118. Lifting point
119. Rudder cable
120. Elevator cables
121. First-aid pack
122. Air bottles
123. Fuselage access panel
124. Bottom keel (connector stringer)

137. Undercarriage electrical interlock
138. Wing horizontal pin forward pick-up
139. Undercarriage retraction jack mechanism
140. Undercarriage pivot bevel
141. 66-Imperial gallon (300-liter) Rüstsatz-3 metal drop tank
142. Mainwheel leg fairing
143. Mainwheel oleo leg
144. Brake lines
145. Mainwheel fairing
146. Port mainwheel
147. Leading-edge skin
148. Port mainwheel well
149. Wing spar
150. Slap actuating linkage
151. Fabric-covered control surfaces
152. Slotted flap structure
153. Leading edge slot-actuating mechanism
154. Slot equalizer rod
155. Handley Page automatic leading edge slot
156. Wing stringers
157. Spar flange decrease
158. Wing ribs
159. Flush-riveted stressed wing skinning
160. Metal framed Frise-type aileron
161. Fixed trim tab
162. Wingtip construction
163. Port navigation light
164. Angled pitot head
165. Rüstsatz-6 optional underwing cannon gondola
166. 14-point plug connection
167. Electrical junction box
168. Cannon rear mounting bracket 20-mm Mauser MG 151/20 cannon
169. Cannon front-mounting bracket
170. Ammunition feed chute
171. Ammunition magazine drum
172. Underwing panel
173. Gondola fairing
174. Cannon barrel

This peculiar juxtaposition spliced together a tall-tailed Bf 109F-1 airframe with a Jumo 213E-1 radial and Fw 190-like cowl, spinner, and propeller. Designated the Bf 209, the fighter variant began development in 1943, when the Focke-Wulf fighter showed lackluster performance at high altitude. When the Fw 190's problems were later overcome, the Bf 209 idea was shelved. *Bowers Collection*

Modifications to the engine sought more power, at high altitudes and otherwise. The DB 605 had a water-methanol injection system, called MW 50, that injected a water-methanol mix into the supercharger to boost

horsepower from 1,450 to as much as 1,800 for multiple boosts lasting at most 10 minutes each. The mix was stowed in a 31-gallon tank aft of the pilot seat.

Two changes came late in the production: the fin and rudder were made slimmer and slightly taller to help prevent the characteristic swing to port on takeoff. Early Gustavs shared the same tail as Friedrichs, but with the G-5 and G-6 the fin and rudder were made slightly taller—135 millimeters or about 5 1/4 inches. The modification also brought a rudder tab, and the rudder was given a straight hinge instead of the angled top.

Following the Gustav pattern of pressurized and nonpressurized cockpits, the G-5 and G-6 were identical except that the G-6 had a nonpressurized cabin. The G-6 also had the tiny air scoops under the oblique windows of the canopy. The G-5 and G-6 were produced simultaneously on the assembly line, until the G-5 was phased out. After the G-5's production run, the G-6 was modified with subsequent changes. The most visible of these later changes was the new slender-framed Erla Haube canopy that replaced the heavy frame and small, sliding side windows with a large single pane on each side. Underwing-mounted air-to-air rockets were tried, but didn't find much operational use.

In summary, the changes that came with G-5 and G-6 included:

Bf 109G-5 and G-6 Specifications

Dimensions—Wingspan: 32 feet, 6 1/2 inches. Length: 29 feet, 8 inches. Height: 8 feet, 2 1/2 inches.

Weight—Empty: 5,900 pounds. Gross: 7,500 pounds.

Powerplant—G-5: Daimler-Benz DB 605D inverted V-12, liquid-cooled engine. Takeoff horsepower: 1,450. G-6: Daimler-Benz DB 605AS. Takeoff horsepower: 1,450.

Armament—G-5: One engine-mounted 20mm MG 151/20 cannon and two MG 131 machine guns, mounted above the engine in the cowl. G-6: One engine-mounted 30mm Rheinmetall-Borsig MK 108 short-barrel cannon (or 20mm Mauser MG 151/20 cannon) and two 13mm MG 131 machine guns, mounted above the cowl.

Performance—Maximum speed: 386 miles per hour at 22,640 feet. Maximum range: 348 miles. Ceiling: 37,900 feet.

- The larger main and tail-wheels introduced with the G-3 became standard.
- A shortened antenna mast and FuG 25a IFF radio equipment.
- DF loop just behind the radio mast.
- Cowl-mounted 13mm MG 131 machine guns.
- A simpler upper cowl (easier and cheaper to produce) that used machine-punched gun troughs instead of separate pieces inserted.
- A taller rudder with a straight hinge.
- A rubber dust cover over the tail-wheel opening.
- A tiny scoop on the MG 131 bulge to help cool the generator.

G-8 (Reconnaissance)

The G-8 was a short-range reconnaissance aircraft that shared the G-6 airframe and powerplants, either DB 605A-1 or DB 605AS. The cowl-mounted MG 131 machine guns were eliminated, but the engine-mounted 30mm MK 108 was retained. (Some G-8s had an engine-mounted 20mm MG 151 instead.) The G-8 had one or two cameras mounted on the underside of the fuselage (either Rb 12,5/7 or Rb 32/7). There was also a gun camera on the leading edge of the port wing, aimable through the gunsight.

G-12 Trainer

Fewer than 100 two-seat trainers were converted from other Gustav nonpressurized versions. Regardless of the version converted—G-2, G-4, and G-6—the designation of the trainer was G-12. Those selected for conversion were typically war-weary aircraft relegated to training units. Consequently, specifications varied according to the version chosen for conversion to trainer. Some were built on assembly lines starting in late 1943.

The Luftwaffe Training Command became desperate for qualified pilots after the terrible losses over Russia and North Africa, and later in the West. With reduced training time and little gas for solo time, the command thought a two-seater would help expedite the training process, which had been cut from a 50-hour flight time before the war to 30. Plus, student flight time in Bf 108s no longer

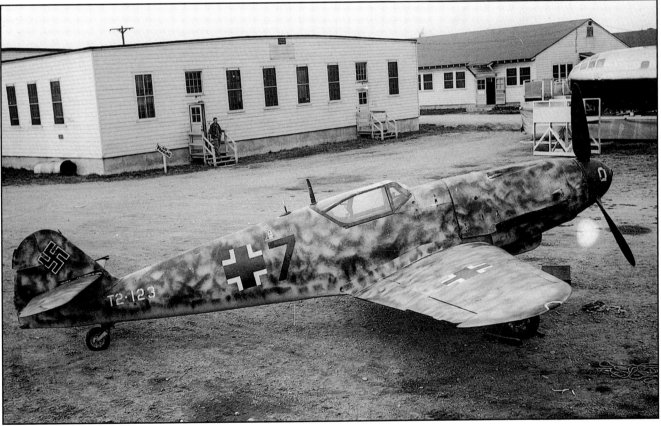

The last of the main production series: the Bf 109K. It entered combat in late fall 1944. Based on the Bf 109G-10, the K was a committee's idea of how to standardize the various basic airframes in use in fall 1944. Visible changes on the K-4 include a raised cowl just in front of the windscreen, a larger tail-wheel, and two protruding trim tabs added to the rudder. Note also the reshaped tail—rounded on top with a more reclined leading edge on the fin and the rear edge of the rudder more vertical, compared to earlier versions. Ks were powered by DB 605ASC or DB 605DC engines, rated at 2,000 horsepower at takeoff. Only about 700 K-4s were believed to have been built by the end of hostilities. This aircraft was brought to Patterson Field in the United States after the war. *Bowers Collection*

Desperate ideas for a desperate nation. A project called *Beethoven*, and later *Mistel*, mounted a Bf 109 or Fw 190 on a Junkers Ju 88 bomber. This example shows a Bf 109F-4 piggybacking on a Ju 88C at Nordhausen airfield. The idea was for the control ship (the fighter on top) to bring the pilotless lower aircraft laden with some 7,700 pounds of explosives to a point where it would detach, then send it crashing into the target via remote control. A similar idea was tried in a United States' experiment that sent B-24s aloft packed with explosives (but no attached fighter) and a single pilot who was to bail out once airborne; the bomber then would be remote controlled to target by an accompanying aircraft (the experiment killed Navy pilot Joseph Kennedy, eldest brother of John F. Kennedy). *Mistel* saw no better success than U.S. attempts. Numerous aircraft were configured this way, but before most could be launched, they were either captured intact when Nordhausen's airfield fell or were destroyed in P-38 strafing raids on Leipzig-Mockau airfield. *Bowers Collection*

gave adequate simulation of the later Bf 109Gs' vicious flight characteristics.

G-10

Following the pattern of the Gustav numbering system, odd numbers designated the fighters with pressurized cabins and even numbers designated those without. Since pressurized cabins stopped being produced after the G-5, the G-10 was intended to follow the G-6 and G-8, but production delays kept it from introduction until early fall 1944, and after the G-14.

With the DB 605D engine with 1,450 horsepower, the G-10 was the fastest of the Gustavs. The G-10 was supposed to standardize that engine (no alternatives as in previous versions), as well as standardizing other equipment that had seen on-and-off use through the Gustavs:

- A Revi 16B reflector sight on a folding bracket (replacing the Revi 12C or 12D).
- Erla Haube canopy that allowed better visibility to the sides and back.
- Taller wooden tail.
- FuG 25a IFF (with DF loop) and FuG 16ZY with a post on the underside of the left wing.

Along with the DB 605D came:

- A refined cowling, including a low bulge on each side of the cowl.
- Wider propeller blades.
- Larger supercharger and air intake.

A succession of G-10 variants were designed for various uses: G-10/R-1 *Jabo* (with ventral bomb rack for one

250-kilogram or four 50-kilogram bombs), G-10/U-2 (with the so-called "Galland" armor-plated hood replaced by framed armor-glass for all-around visibility; two MG 131s and three MK 108s), G-10/R-2 (reconnaissance; two MG 131s and one MK 108), and others. All had the DB 605D powerplant.

G-14 (Pressurized Cabin)

The G-14 was introduced before the G-10, while the G-10 waited for the Daimler-Benz DB 605D. The G-14 continued using the DB 605A engine. The G-14 was a catchall that standardized some of the same features of preceding Gustavs, but retained the DB 605AM or DB 605AS (with enlarged supercharger). Standardized features included:

- The so-called "Galland" hood replaced by framed *panzerglas* for all-around visibility.
- Armor-protected radiator and oil cooler.
- A small air scoop to cool the generator, and a bulge for the larger oil pump.
- A fixed tail-wheel (usually with a longer leg).

Most were fitted on the assembly line with the drop tank rack under the designation G-14/R-3. A metal tail assembly was standard but those designated Bf 109G-14/U-4 had a wooden tail assembly. Like the G-10, there was a long line of subvariants for specific purposes.

Bf 109K

The K version represented the Third Reich's last production version of the Bf 109. The letters *I* and *J* were skipped (*I* not used to avoid confusion with "variants of a basic design" and *J* because Hispano-built models already used the letter). The new series was an attempt to simplify Bf 109 production, which had become unwieldy and confusing with so many subtly different variants.

The first Ks appeared in late fall 1944. Externally, they looked much like the G-10. They also used the MW 50 and GM 1 injection systems. Standard features included:

- The "Galland" hood with its all-around pilot visibility.
- Enlarged wooden tail assembly.
- Larger mainwheels (with bulges necessitated on the upper wing surfaces) and tail-wheel (semiretractable with doors).
- Mainwheel covers (frequently removed by line units).
- Two external trim tabs on the rudder.

The K-4 was the only version of the K-series produced in any significant number—about 700 total aircraft. K-4s and K-6s were identical except the K-6 had a 30mm cannon gondola mounted under each wing. These served

---

Bf 109K-4 Specifications

Dimensions—Wingspan: 32 feet, 8 1/2 inches. Length: 29 feet, 1/2 inch. Height: 8 feet, 2 1/2 inches.

Weight—Empty: 4,886 pounds. Gross: 7,440 pounds.

Powerplant—Daimler-Benz DB 605ASCM inverted V-12, liquid-cooled engine. Takeoff horsepower: 1,475.

Armament—One 20mm Mk. 103 or Mk. 108 engine-mounted cannon and two 15mm Mauser MG 151s, mounted above the engine in the cowl.

Performance—Maximum speed: 452 miles per hour at 19,700 feet. Maximum range: 356 miles. Ceiling: 41,000 feet.

---

in various units, including JG 3, 4, 11, 27, 51, 52, 53, and 77. The K-2 was also produced but in lesser number; it differed from the K-4 only in that the K-4 had a pressurized cabin and the K-2 did not. Many versions of the K series were planned, but few were fabricated. The K was the final in long succession of production series, continuing until May 1945, when unconditional surrender ended the war in Europe.

Variants

During the middle years of the war, several special-use Bf 109s were created but saw only the prototype stage or a very short production run. Among these was the Bf 109H version, made for high-altitude reconnaissance. To this end, wingspan was extended with a center section spliced into the Gustav's wing panels, giving a wingspan of 39 feet 1 1/2 inches. Tail surfaces were increased proportionately. Landing gear was spread, being attached outside the underwing radiators instead of the fuselage/wing root area. It had a service ceiling of 47,900 feet. It was completed from G-5 airframes and carried the same equipment internally. A very few were built, in early 1944.

The Bf 209 program attempted to marry the Bf 109F-1 airframe with a Jumo 213E-1 radial engine. The result looked like a Fw 190 spliced together with a Bf 109. By spring 1944, the prototype was ready for flight testing, but success in overcoming the faults of Fw 190 at high altitudes brought an end to the program.

Another variant had tricycle landing gear and mainwheels spread at about the same width as the H version. This concept came to be called the Bf 309 and saw prototypes but no production machines.

CHAPTER 7

OVER SAND DUNES AND SNOW DRIFTS

In early 1941, it was a foregone conclusion to Bf 109 pilots that, given their current strength, they could not annihilate the RAF and open the way for invasion of England. That's when *Reichsmarschall* Göring delivered astonishing news to an audience of air unit commanders gathered in Paris from across occupied France. Göring announced that a renewed campaign against Great Britain would bring "immensely increased rearmament of the Air Force, an intensification of the U-boat war, and would be brought to a conclusion by the actual invasion itself." Supremely confident as always, the portly *Reichsmarschall* talked at length about what would be done and how it would be done, building to a rousing conclusion. Surprised as anyone in the room, Adolf Galland noted: "The plans Göring unfolded before us were convincing. . . ."

As the stunned commanders filed out of the briefing room, Göring stood "beaming" and motioned for Galland and Werner Mölders. After asking what they thought of his "performance," he leaned closer and intimated: "there's not a grain of truth in it."

It was all a ruse to cover a plan requiring such secrecy that even Luftwaffe commanders were not privy to the truth: Operation *Seelöwe* was long dead. Instead would be Operation *Barbarossa*, the invasion of the Soviet Union. Galland was stunned speechless by the prospect.

"The dread which had been hanging over us like the sword of Damocles since the beginning of the war would now become a reality: war on two fronts," Galland commented. "I could think of nothing else but the dark and sinister vision of starting a war with the Soviet Union, so tremendously strong in manpower and natural resources, while our strength had already proved insufficient to conquer the British in the first assault. Now we were to turn against a new, unknown and in any case, gigantic enemy. . . ."

Operation *Barbarossa* was monstrous in scope beyond what anyone in modern history had ever dared conceive. The Wehrmacht would need to muster three million men and 2,000 Luftwaffe combat aircraft in an attempt to cover a front 870 miles long, from the Balkans to the Black Sea.

Before invasion of the Soviet Union, however, Germany had business to finish in North Africa, Malta, and the Balkans. Success of the Bf 109 was central to all of it.

Desert 109s

The Bf 109 became the aerial mainstay supporting Rommel's Afrika Korps in the see-saw clashes of the desert. The little fighter vacillated between an offensive and defensive role, depending on the swing

Under North Africa's brutal sun and suffocating heat, cockpit controls literally became too hot to touch. Hence, a common sight is the beach umbrella. *Black 8* displays some personal artwork (*Jagdgeschwadern* unknown) and the 87-octane triangle, meaning standard fuel and a standard DB 605 engine in this Gustav. *Bowers Collection*

of the momentum on the ground. Momentum would shift for and against Rommel many times over two years.

When Rommel's Heinkel 111 first landed in North Africa on February 12, 1941, Italian forces had their backs against the wall. Troops were plunging in headlong retreat toward Tripoli, with the British Commonwealth troops in hot pursuit. Rommel's great challenge was to turn the situation around.

The vanguard of his Afrika Korps, the Fifth Light Division, arrived two days later. Soon after, a *Stukageschwadern* accompanied by Bf 110s arrived, and it would be two months before Bf 109s would come in force.

Rommel's first major offensive began on March 31. In support of the clanking, dust-churning panzers were Ju 87 Stukas. An attack on British-held El Agheila was successful, and the Afrika Korps went on to a succession of dazzling victories that included the capture of Benghazi, where the British had been ordered to take a firm stand but failed. Success in the air was mixed however. The Stukas, supported by Bf 110 *Zerstörers*, were vulnerable to the attacking RAF fighters, as had been proven so forcefully in the Battle of Britain.

On April 14, 1941, elements of I/JG 27 touched down on African sands for the first time at their new and (what would become relatively longstanding) home field at El Gazala in Libya. Concurrent with the fighters' arrival was a visit by Erhard Milch, who bestowed an airman's compliment on Rommel describing him as "one of our more air-minded generals." Rommel recognized the Bf 109 as a formidable weapon that he would exploit in his brilliant strategies.

However, during much of his North African campaign, Rommel had to "share" his Bf 109s for other Mediterranean activities, namely the aerial offensive against the island fortress of Malta, staunchly held by the British. If captured, Malta's strategic location in the Mediterranean Sea would enable the Luftwaffe to interdict British shipping.

Large-scale bomber strikes against Malta required Bf 109 escorts to confront Malta-based RAF Hurricanes and

Hans-Joachim Marseille, a legend among German aviators. At the age of 22, after barely a year of combat, he scored his 158th credited victory (151 in Africa). He won all while piloting Bf 109s. The first came on his third sortie after he came to the desert in spring 1941. He flew a total of 382 missions, before being killed in a flight accident with a defective G-2 on September 30, 1942. This photo was taken earlier the same month, on September 4. *National Archives*

Gladiator interceptors. In February, the same month that Rommel arrived in Africa, a dozen Bf 109Es of 7./JG 26 landed on Sicily to begin their seven-month mission against Malta. Later in 1941, the top-scoring *Jagdgeschwader*, JG 53, with four *Gruppen* of Bf 109Fs, was also stationed in Sicily for operations against Malta, as well as to escort transports on their way to Africa. (Malta never did fall, and eventually the *Gruppen* based in Sicily either were sent to the Russian front or joined the fighter forces in Africa.)

Meanwhile, African-based Bf 109s in tandem with Stukas proved to be extraordinarily effective against the British land army. Many of the fighters at Sicily were Bf 109Fs, but the older Emils of JG 27 were deemed adequate for North Africa—and proved more than a match for the RAF aircraft stationed there at that time.

The Emils' first skirmish on April 19 was successful: They shot down four Hurricanes of RAF No. 274 Squadron and lost one of their own. The rest of I/JG 27 arrived a few days later, bringing the *Gruppe* to full strength.

The desert was a unique environment for fighting men on the ground and in the air. This was the Western Desert, also known as the Libyan Desert—one of the harshest environments on earth. Temperatures here could reach 136 degrees Fahrenheit at midday and often dropped to below freezing at night.

Wind-propelled sand was almost constant. It had such a fine consistency that it penetrated even sealed dashboard instruments. It sandblasted the camouflage paint from aircraft surfaces and, worst of all, it could cut the operating life of engines by half.

The Bf 109 stood up to desert conditions better than one might expect. To extend engine life, "tropicalization" included installation of a box-like air filter (later filters were canister-shaped) that attached to the supercharger intake along the cowl's port side. Tropicalized aircraft also carried an emergency desert survival pack with provisions and a carbine tucked into the "baggage area" behind the pilot seat.

Returning from a *Freie Jagd* on British armor, this Bf 109E of I/JG 27 descends toward the hot desert sands. Inland, the North African desert is wide, open, and flat—good for field expedient airstrips and also riding out a crash landing, if necessary. *Ethell Collection*

Maintenance of the Daimler-Benz engine had to be performed in the open air, but the "black men" took care as much as possible to prevent abrasive sand and grit from reaching the engine's internal parts.

The nature of air combat in the desert was unique, and fighter pilots adjusted their tactics to fit the environment. It was the land of *Freie Jagd*. There was less structured flight, and greater freedom in air-to-ground attack. When not escorting the Ju 87s and 88s, the fighters were at liberty to roam a wide expanse where enemy columns and supply dumps and airfields could spring up almost anywhere, and were visible from great distances for lack of any kind of ground cover. *Freie Jagd* sorties allowed searches for these targets, which often inflicted great, sudden devastation on the enemy. There were no civilian dwellings or population to distract or confuse with military targets. So virtually anything not known to be German was fair game for prowling Bf 109s.

In the brilliant blue sky, bright sunshine was a constant (on average, there is 3,000 hours of sunshine per year in the Western Desert). So, what better place for the old dogfighting tactic of swooping down out of the blinding sun with guns blazing on targets in the air or on the ground?

Navigation could be challenging. Just south of the Mediterranean coast is the "Great Sand Sea." Flying over it truly was like flying over the sea—an uncharted expanse with no cities and no rivers or other features as guides.

On June 1, I/JG 27 was reinforced with six more E-7s of 7/JG 26, which arrived in North Africa from Sicily when their Malta mission ended. Two weeks later, on June 15, Commonwealth forces launched a major offensive they code-named Operation *Battleaxe*. A heavy air attack also ensued, led by RAF Hurricanes. Bf 109s went into action protecting the German armored columns. Against this offensive, the German 88mm antiaircraft gun was also used with devastating effect—not attacking aircraft, but as an antitank weapon. On June 17, Rommel launched a counterattack that sent Commonwealth forces reeling.

Britain's *Battleaxe* had failed, but with the invasion of the Soviet Union on June 22, Rommel would receive no reinforcements or new equipment to press his advantage. Priority for amassing weapons went to the Russian front. No fighter reinforcements would come until September 1941, when II/JG 27 landed in Africa. With the unit came the new Bf 109F, the first Friedrichs to arrive in Africa. (Emils would remain in service in other units as *Jabos* and reconnaissance fighters throughout much of 1942.)

In early November 1941, just in time for another British offensive called operation *Crusader*, III/JG 27 also relocated from Sicily to Africa to reunite with I and II *Gruppen*, making *Jagdgeschwader* 27 whole for the first time in more than 18 months. III *Gruppe* also was equipped with Bf 109Fs.

Launched November 18, *Crusader* brought a renewed Allied air offensive, coming at a time when resupply was a problem for the Luftwaffe. Fuel stores had become low because of constant Allied attacks on Italian shipping across the Mediterranean.

With *Crusader* also came catastrophic rains that blotted out the desert's expansive blue sky with inky black clouds. Furious rain caused sudden torrential rivers with currents so swift that they carried away tents, equipment, and even disabled aircraft. El Gazala in particular became a quagmire of shifting sands churned up by moving water. Before they were trapped there, all serviceable Bf 109s fled El Gazala for drier ground at the temporary station at Martuba. In the meantime, the Allies gained ground, and by the time El Gazala dried out, it was in the RAF's hands.

JG 27 and elements of JG 26 engaged Commonwealth fighter forces repeatedly in November. On November 20, South African Air Force Marylands attempted to attack Rommel's columns, but I/JG 27 scrambled and promptly downed 4 without losing any. On November 22, Bf 109Fs from II and III/JG 27 confronted RAF Tomahawks, Hurricanes, and Blenheims, downing 10 of the fighters and 4 of the Blenheims, but losing 6 Bf 109Fs in the process. With Hitler's priorities elsewhere, these were slow to be replaced.

In early December, III/JG 53 also relocated from Sicily and found a temporary home on the coast at Derna. Rapid reverses in the fast-moving desert war forced Rommel's

A cripple caught on the ground. This Bf 109G-2/Trop falls intact into the hands of advancing Allied forces, during one of the many surges and retreats of the desert war. It would be checked carefully for booby traps then turned over for testing. *Ethell Collection*

retreat and a consequential abandonment of Derna before Christmas. Losing primitive "bases"—little more than firm, flat stretches—was not a major setback, because the capture of open desert territory was not Rommel's objective any more than naval fleets "capture" open stretches of sea. But abandoning a number of Bf 109Fs under repair in a swift pullout was a significant loss. Many times in the North African campaign, fighters had to pull back and consolidate on German-held territory, then continue operations before moving forward again as Rommel drove the enemy back.

By February 1942, the same problem of overstretched supply lines that had frustrated Rommel on his advances now tethered the British as well. Lacking the means to rearm, refuel, and reequip, *Crusader* lost its initial momentum and trudged to a halt. Then Rommel went on the offensive again, sending the British reeling beyond Derna all the way back to El Gazala. Contributing to the rout was the newly arrived II/JG 53, fresh from Sicily, to join its contingent in El Gazala in protection of the Stukas and other bombers.

A lull followed until spring, when Rommel finally broke through the Gazala line on the way to his long-awaited prize of Tobruk. When Rommel sent his panzers

marauding in the last week of May, the Bf 109s did some marauding of their own. Thirty-nine RAF fighters were shot down between May 29 and May 31, despite the arrival of the new Spitfire Mk. V by this time.

Rommel shattered the brave defenders of Tobruk and recaptured it in June with help from his air support. As Rommel rolled on eastward, Stukas were used extensively to attack the retreating British. Although effective against slow-moving ground targets, Stukas were easy prey for virtually any RAF fighter. So Bf 109s temporarily refrained from *Freie Jagd* to escort the vulnerable dive-bombers.

It was during the torrid months of 1942 that many German pilots joined the ranks of aces, but one Bf 109 pilot shone above the rest: Christened the "Star of Africa," Hans-Joachim Marseille of III/JG 27 made his meteoric rise, shooting down a total of 158 aircraft—all but seven in North Africa—during little more than a year as a combat pilot. Making this score even more phenomenal was the fact that all but four of his victories were over enemy fighters. Besides being an outstanding pilot, Marseille was an outstanding marksman, able to fire deflection (off-angle) shots with deadly accuracy.

The staggering tally of 158 over such a short time would rise no higher because, on September 30, 1942, while flying on routine patrol in one of the first Bf 109G-2s in North Africa, Marseille noticed wisps of oily smoke in the cockpit. As a mysterious engine fire grew worse, he soon realized he had to bail out. He climbed up out of the cockpit and was flung back into the slipstream. He sustained a broad chest wound when he struck the tail. His limp body plummeted to the desert sand and he was buried at the spot. Galland described Marseille as "the unrivaled virtuoso among the fighter pilots of the Second World War."

The untimely death of the Bf 109's "unrivaled virtuoso" seemed to foreshadow the demise of Rommel's *Panzerarmee Afrika*. It too had seemed to possess unlimited promise, as Rommel geared up for yet another push. Fighter forces had been strengthened further with the addition of II/JG 26, relocated from France. With an umbrella of fighters overhead, Rommel's panzers made a lunge for the last major stronghold between his forces and the Suez Canal: El Alamein.

Here, he clashed with the greatly reinforced British Eighth Army, now led by the newly appointed British Lieutenant General Bernard Montgomery. Rommel's forces were soundly beaten at El Alamein. On the heels of that defeat came operation *Torch*—the Anglo-American assault that would finish Rommel in its great pincers.

In November 1942, forces under Lieutenant General Dwight D. Eisenhower landed at French-held northwest Africa. The Americans brought a profusion of equipment such as Africa had never seen—beyond the wildest dreams of threadbare British and Germans alike. This offered the *Jagdgeschwadern* lots of new targets in the air and on the ground, but also greater opposition than ever. An air-to-ground attack might bring a barrage of defensive fire from all directions, from sources seen and unseen. Bf 109 pilot Jürgen Harder, *Oberleutnant* in JG 53 later described the target-rich environment of the desert and its increased hazards:

> A wild hunt developed for everything that moved down below—tanks, reconnaissance vehicles, cars, trucks, motorcycles, infantry columns. One *Schwarm* attacked a train on the railway near the road. Without braking, the engineer jumped from the locomotive and ran away across the fields. Soon, however, the train stopped as it was badly hit, and the rail line began to climb. Shortly before the end of the road I zoomed upward to 200 meters to see if I had hit a particular vehicle, when there was a loud bang in my cockpit. There was a large hole in the left side window through which the airstream entered. The left side of my face was covered with blood and blood was also flowing from my left hand. The instrument panel was completely destroyed. I (radioed): 'am slightly wounded—flying home.' I flew back without any engine control, but performed a good landing.

With German ground forces on the run, airfields could not be held. Fighter units were withdrawn or captured. Inevitably, with endless resources heaped against them, Rommel's ground forces in Africa retreated until they had no where else to go. British and American army pincers sliced through the *Panzerarmee*'s weak flanks and surrounded 200,000 German troops by mid-May 1943. The Axis threat in Africa was vanquished.

Bf 109s in Support of the Balkans Invasion

In the spring of 1941, while Rommel's North African campaign still raged, Hitler concluded angrily that he would have to invade the Balkan nations of Greece and Yugoslavia. He didn't want to. He wanted stability in the Balkans during the launch of operation *Barbarossa*, not another front to spread his forces thinner.

Italian dictator Benito Mussolini had forced Hitler's hand. To redeem the prestige of the Axis and to keep his bungling Italian partner solvent after repeated defeats, Hitler intervened.

What perturbed Hitler most about Mussolini's bungling aggression was that it brought the British back to the continent, as Winston Churchill fulfilled his well-publicized pledge to send military help to the Greeks in the event of invasion. Four Commonwealth divisions (otherwise badly needed to fight Rommel in North Africa) had occupied Crete and the Aegean island of Lemnos. Perhaps most threatening and certainly most pertinent to the Bf 109's story was the fact that the RAF stationed wings at airfields in southern Greece, threatening air attack on Romania's Ploesti oilfields, which provided fuel essential for Hitler's Luftwaffe and panzer units.

As it turned out, the Luftwaffe was well prepared for the new threat—thanks to strategic planning that massed some 400 combat aircraft around the vital oilfields. Romania was already a Nazi satellite and Bulgaria was lately coerced into becoming one as well. In March 1941, Bulgaria invited German air and ground forces into staging areas near the border with its despised neighbor, Greece. Many aircraft moved into convenient striking distance. Moved to forward fields in Romania were elements of JG 54, JG 27, JG 77, as well as *Jagdgruppen* from LG 2. All were equipped with Bf 109Es.

On April 6, 1941, the Luftwaffe bombers and fighters rose from eight forward airfields into a cloudless dawn. Escorting waves of Ju 87s and 88s, some Bf 109s flew along with their charges south to targets in Greece, while others winged west toward the Yugoslavian capitol of Belgrade.

On the way to Belgrade, planes with familiar square-tipped wings of the Yugoslavian Sixth Fighter Regiment were frantically taking off to confront the attackers in what became a bizarre and brief battle in the air. With recent German aircraft sales, the Yugoslavs also flew *Emils*!

About 60 were in service, although many were caught on the ground. Those that got airborne had an even fight, one-on-one, but the odds quickly turned in favor of the swarming Luftwaffe.

After a short foray, the attackers flew on to the Yugoslav capitol leaving a trail of crashed Emils with Yugoslav markings. Like in the merciless attack on Warsaw, much of Belgrade was pummeled into dust. With as many as 17,000 dead in the city alone, and key command and communication lines shattered throughout, Yugoslavian forces were brought to their knees in a week.

Greece-bound Bf 109s faced the small Greek air force, along with a small contingent of the RAF Hurricanes, Gladiators, and Blenheims. Those that managed to get airborne were quickly overwhelmed. That opened the door for German panzers and other ground forces to stream through mountain passes to overwhelm the Greek army and mountain irregulars who had valiantly driven back the Italians. A high priority of the Luftwaffe was to finish off surviving aircraft at the large air base near Piraeus, where the new RAF arrivals were based.

On April 20, all 15 Hurricanes on Piraeus' field scrambled into the skies of southern Greece to meet the approaching Luftwaffe. The sky was dotted with more than 100 Ju 88s, with Bf 109s and 110s swarming above. Bf 109s scored five victories over the Hurricanes that day and the remaining 10 were shot up so badly that some were written off after limping back to base. On April 23, the few surviving aircraft of the Greek air force and RAF were evacuated to Crete.

While German ground forces had Greek and British infantry on the run, Bf 109s flew unopposed and harassed the retreating troops. In desperation not known since Dunkirk, the British ordered evacuation of forces from the tip of Greece to the bastion of Crete. Greece surrendered on April 27.

In the Balkan blitzkrieg, 54 Bf 109Es were shot down, compared to 110 Greek, British, and Yugoslavian fighters claimed as aerial victories by Bf 109 and 110 crews.

The next German objective became Crete. To soften its formidable defenses, a force of He 111s and Ju 88s escorted by Bf 109s was sent to attack Crete's harbors. RAF Hurricanes and Gladiators lifted off Crete's air base to intercept. Bf 109s ravaged them, leaving only seven fighters in defense. By May 19, virtually uncontested airspace was won once again. This contributed to the success of two Bf

Bomb loaders ratchet up a 250-kilogram (552.5-pound) bomb on a hand-operated bomb lift to arm this Bf 109F-4/R-6 *Jabo*. Note the hand crank of the inertia starter and the thick p*anzerglas* of the windscreen. *Bowers Collection*

A Gustav is prepared with a 250-kilogram (552.5-pound) payload to pound Russian defenses. The emblem on the cowl identifies this aircraft as being from JG 3 Udet. *Bowers Collection*

109E *Jabos* that slipped through screens to reach Royal Navy ships tasked with protecting Crete. The two *Jabos* dropped 500-pound bombs on the British cruiser HMS *Fiji*, which later capsized and sunk. Crete was overrun by June 2, 1941, but at a terrible price to German airborne divisions.

Bf 109s at the Russian Front

With the Balkans now under control, Hitler could finally launch Operation *Barbarossa*. The lure of the Soviet Union's vast resources and *lebensraum* (living space) would be Hitler's undoing.

The Luftwaffe's first attack was timed to coincide with a tremendous artillery barrage precisely at 3:15 A.M. on June 22, 1941. Committed to the first strike were 637 He 111 and Ju 88 bombers, with the specific mission of destroying 66 forward airfields identified by Luftwaffe reconnaissance. Escorting them were 231 Bf 109s. These were the vanguard from a total of 440 Bf 109s availed initially for the operation. A full third of these were older Emils and the rest were new Friedrichs.

Fighter units were assigned to sectors corresponding to the invading German divisions: II/JG 54 in the northern sector; II and III/JG 27 in the central sector; and I and II/JG 52, II and II/JG 77 and I (*Jadg*)/LG 2 in the southern sector.

The Luftwaffe swarmed over the Russian fields crowded with neatly parked aircraft. While surprised Soviet pilots desperately strapped in to confront the attackers, hangars and aircraft were exploding around them.

The besieged Russians flew an array of aircraft that included old I-16 Ratas, the familiar and nominal nemesis from the Spanish Civil War, as well as Hawker Hurricanes, American-built Bell P-39 Airacobras, and Curtiss P-40 Kittyhawks.

The first confirmed air-to-air victory of *Barbarossa* is credited to 4./JG 3's *Staffelkapitan*, Robert Olejnik, at 3:58 A.M. Piloting a Bf 109F-2, Olejnik took off at 3:30

A.M. from a Polish airstrip only 30 miles from Soviet territory. He later recalled: "I took off with my *Rottenflieger* to reconnoiter Russian airfields near the border, watching for enemy fighters. As I got nearer I saw that two aircraft were already manned by pilots. At a height of 700–800 meters I flew a wide turn round the airfield and watched closely. After one and half circuits, I saw the Russians start their engines and taxi out, then take off immediately. . . . I attacked the first 'Rata' with a height advantage of 300–400 meters, and succeeded in shooting it down with only a few rounds in my first attack."

That was the first of 322 Russian aircraft shot out of the sky during the carnage of the first day of *Barbarossa*. Destruction of parked aircraft was more than fourfold—1,489 destroyed on the ground. These figures were consistent with the Russian count.

Luftwaffe losses were incredibly low: 35 total. Among the few Bf 109 pilots lost were Wolfgang Schellmann, *Kommodore* of JG 27 (26 total victories, including some in Spain) and *Hauptmann* Heinz Bretnutz of II/JG 53 (27 victories). Schellmann's Bf 109 had been damaged by flying debris of a disintegrating I-16 Rata, his 26th victory. He was forced to bail out and was captured near Grodno. As a portent to the fate of many other fliers downed over Russia, Schellmann was executed by the *NKVD* two days later.

Soviet forward fields were so close to the Luftwaffe's fields in Poland that many crews landed, rearmed, refueled and lifted off for sorties *eight* times on the first day. The Red Air Force retaliatory attempts against the Luftwaffe's forward bases failed miserably.

After only a week, the Germans announced they had destroyed 4,017 enemy aircraft with a loss of only *150 of their own*—tallies the Soviets could only grimly acknowledge and did not dispute.

These crippling losses temporarily opened the Russian skies for the Luftwaffe to roam freely. Plus, it enabled the juggernaut of panzers and infantry to rampage into the heart of Russia with little fear of attack from the air. The bombers went on to smash communication lines, bridges, and railroads, which delayed the Red Army from regrouping.

As the months went on, the Red Air Force pumped more and more aircraft into the fray, giving Bf 109 pilots a target-rich environment that sent personal scores soaring. At the end of June 1941, the anxious German press kept watch, almost like for a sporting event, for the fall of the aerial record of 80 victories held by the "Red Baron,"

From the harshest torrid climates to the harshest frigid ones, the Bf 109 saw extensive service. At Stalingrad, where hoof-powered sleds were more dependable than trucks, Bf 109s flew from 1941 until the demise of the German Sixth Army in February 1943. This Bf 109F-2 kicks up stinging snow in its prop wash while taxiing to the runway. The chevron on the fuselage indicates a *Staffelkapitan*. Ethell Collection

Manfred von Richthofen, from World War I. With a number of young, aggressive, sure-shot pilots following in the footsteps of Marseille, a dark horse conceivably could have suddenly surged into contention. But as it turned out, the veteran Werner Mölders was the only ace to score his 80th before June was over. A couple weeks later, Mölders reached the 100 mark and at the same time, Walter Oesau, *Kommodore* of JG 3 scored his 80th. A long line of distinguished Bf 109 pilots would soon equal and surpass the scores.

The voluminous German victories were not without cost. Large-scale air attacks against Moscow, which Hitler ordered "razed to the ground," as well as the formidable Soviet Baltic fleet, proved very costly, and not very effective. By mid-July, 1,284 Luftwaffe aircraft had been lost or damaged—a number exceeding the original commitment of aircraft at the start of *Barbarossa* four weeks before.

Also by mid-July, panzers in the central sector had surged 400 miles, bringing them within 200 miles of Moscow. Still, strategic points were out of reach, even for the Luftwaffe. Russian war industry cranked up to maximum capacity, increasing aircraft production fourfold, to totals of 15,735 aircraft of all types during 1941. Short-sightedness of German top leadership had created a Luftwaffe that reigned supreme on the tactical front (i.e., with Bf 109s) but was powerless to launch strategic strikes on Soviet production centers, now relocated safely beyond the Luftwaffe's short reach. There had been little invested in development of large, long-range bombers. Göring had

Russians should have known their aerial adversary well, having faced Bf 109s in the Spanish Civil War and having some in their own inventory. Germany had sold five E-3s to Russia in 1939. It is not known if the Germans sold this Bf 109F when the German-Russian Nonaggression Pact was still in effect, or if it was captured by Russian forces later. The F version was introduced about half a year before Germany invaded Russia. *Bowers Collection*

dismissed the idea, saying, *"Der Führer* will want to know how many (bombers), not how big." And the Reich continued to churn out large numbers of Heinkel and Dornier medium bombers, along with Bf 109s (still Germany's only single-seat fighter).

Friedrichs were now in good supply. Losses, battle damage, and everyday wear and tear caused a gradual disappearance of Emils from the front-line *Jagdgeschwadern.* Friedrichs quickly replaced them. Following the initial onslaught of *Barbarossa*, II/JG 27 was pulled off the line to reequip with Bf 109Fs back in Germany. II/JG 52, which also began the campaign with Emils, was now equipped with Bf 109Fs (except for a few surviving Emils as spares). The only Emils remaining in a front-line service were *Jabos*. (As a temporary measure, some Emils were also drawn together for front-line service in early 1942, when JG 5 was formed.)

German ground forces stalled at the onset of severe winter weather in December 1941, and Luftwaffe operations slowed commensurate with it. Some *Jagdgeschwadern* were withdrawn for service in the Mediterranean, including II and II/JG 27 and I, II, and III/JG 53.

The remaining *Jagdgeschwadern* endured one of the harshest winters on record, yet they watched incredulously as the Soviets continued air operations, seemingly impervious to the subzero temperatures that froze German engines and armaments solid. In their native climate, Russian ground crews knew secrets that the Germans would have to learn through trial and error—things as simple as reliquifying congealed engine oil with gasoline (the kerosine or gasoline evaporate at operating temperature) and rinsing lubricants off frozen moving parts of machine guns with gasoline. There were idiosyncrasies unique to the Bf 109 in winter, too, like the need to remove mainwheel covers to avoid snow buildup that could lock the wheels tight in landing and takeoff.

With the thaw in the spring of 1942, the fighting heated up, reaching new peaks in ferocity and numbers committed to battle. Among the German objectives was the capture of the strategic Black Sea port of Sevastopol on the Crimea peninsula. Ground troops numbering 210,000 and *Luftflotte* 4 were hurled against the city. Ju 87s and 88s, He 111s and escorting Bf 109Fs struck furiously.

JG 52 and JG 77 in particular helped clear the skies for a decisive victory that captured the port and city. Sevastopol was a textbook example of an integrated air-ground campaign. The 30-day siege required an incredible 23,751 sorties that cost an inordinately small 31 aircraft. But that would be the last time Bf 109s would clear the skies so decisively over Russia.

The Russians had begun to close the gap in aircraft performance with the introduction of the Yak-9 and others in late 1942. But by early 1943, Gustavs were outfitting front-line *Geschwadern*, after introduction the previous October. The clearly superior Gustavs once again extended the lead over the best Yaks, but the sheer volume of Russian aircraft gradually became overwhelming. It seemed to the Luftwaffe pilots that for every Russian fighter knocked down, another two materialized to replace it.

Hitler insisted that he would capture Stalingrad, or destroy it trying. Strategically useless but with a name embodying the Russian spirit, Stalingrad came under pounding, merciless attack by General (later Field Marshal) Friedrich Paulus' Sixth Army. Like the all-out air attack on Sevastopol, the *Fliegerkorps'* 600 aircraft were launched against Stalingrad, which virtually leveled the sprawling city. Then it became a priority for Red Army reinforcement—which turned the tables against the Germans.

Gradually, Red Army units approaching from the northwest and southeast edged around the German Sixth Army's weak flanks and encircled it. Paulus received firm orders from Hitler: "Do not give an inch."

Bf 109s were retained on station inside the huge, noose-like circle as the seething enemy sought to choke the Germans to death. The Luftwaffe launched a desperate effort to resupply trapped Sixth Army troops and the Bf 109s were vital escorts. Protecting the lumbering transports in the brutal weather in winter 1942–1943, the Bf 109s flew hundreds of sorties. Again, the battle of attrition couldn't be won by Germany. The *Jagdgeschwadern* dwindled, Bf 109s being lost one by one agains]t the increasingly superior numbers of Soviet aircraft thrown against them.

On Stalingrad's outskirts, the Germans had established a number of expeditionary airfields, some little more than commandeered tundra. The last of them, Gumrak, fell as the Russian noose pulled tight on January 22, 1943. The last Bf 109 to leave the circle was a G-2 from JG 3, piloted by the sole survivor of an all-volunteer contingent of six that stayed on to do what little they could to fend off Russian air-to-ground attack in the last dark days. On February 2, 1943, the remaining remnants of 300,000 German troops finally laid down their arms. Paulus had surrendered on January 31.

The remaining shreds of *Barbarossa* unraveled from there. A succession of major German defeats followed as the Russian counteroffensive gained momentum. Bf 109s were now covering withdrawals from hard-won territory in Russia, like through the rugged Caucasus region, and trying to stave off attackers from German troops trapped on the Crimea peninsula. There was one more major air victory—called by some the largest air battle of all time: On July 5, 1943, the Battle of Kursk saw 432 Russian aircraft shot down and a loss of only 26 German aircraft.

The Soviet offensive roared forward with vengence unparalleled. Bf 109 units fell back with the German ground units, doing backward leaps as if in a reversed home movie—sometimes occupying the same airfields they used in the advance of 1941. It was clear that Bf 109s reigned supreme in Soviet skies, but attrition and overwhelmed ground forces led to overall defeat.

CHAPTER 8

DEFENSE OF THE FATHERLAND

With forces in North Africa and Russia in shambles, the Third Reich was spiraling down like a fatally stricken Messerschmitt. By the beginning of 1943, Luftwaffe losses were staggering: 2,400 aircraft had been destroyed in North Africa since the battle of El Alamein; on the Russian front, between June 22, 1941, and April 8, 1942, losses numbered 2,951 (out of 850 aircraft dispatched for the Stalingrad airlift, less than half survived). In the meantime, massive bombardment of the Fatherland ensued from the west as the U.S. Eighth Air Force began regular daylight bombing missions and the RAF's Bomber Command found new life with a new leader, Air Marshal Sir Arthur (Bomber) Harris. Bombing began "round the clock."

On January 27, 1943, the USAAF attacked its first target on German soil, Wilhelmshaven, the submarine-building center on the North Sea. Short-legged Spitfires flew patrols in conjunction with the raid but couldn't begin to fly the distance to target alongside the B-17 Flying Fortresses and B-24 Liberators. Losses were not great for either the attacking forces or the defenders, but the point was that the Americans had successfully attacked Germany itself. At this time, units left in defense of the west were JG 1, JG 2, and JG 26.

The bombing ensued day and night. The RAF stepped up night bombing and the USAAF began a regimen of large-scale raids, like on April 17, 1943, when Bremen was pummeled. The need for more fighters to defend the Reich became alarmingly apparent.

Despite the innovations and much more advanced aircraft designs on both the German and Allied sides, the Bf 109 remained the backbone of the fighter forces to the end of the war. War-weary F interceptors shown here were kept in a constant state of readiness, awaiting pilots who would scramble to meet yet another Allied attack. *Bowers Collection*

At left and below:
The shape of things to come. Another Messerschmitt creation: The Messerschmitt 262 jet fighter. With a top speed of 540 miles per hour, it could humble any fighter in the air. It entered the war in the 11th hour, with time to produce only 1,400—too little and too late to turn the tide of Allied bombing.
National Archives

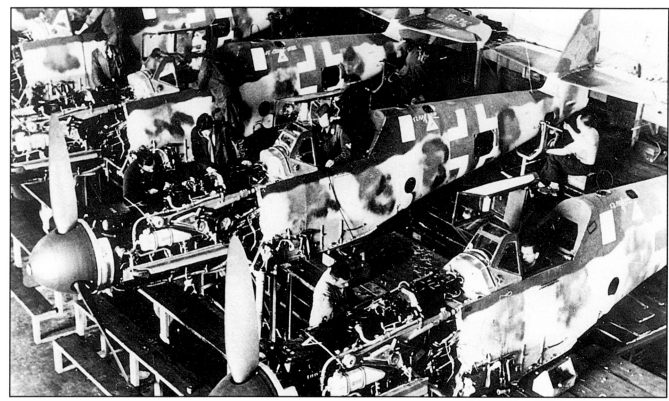

The assembly line at Regensburg. Thanks in part to innovations by Albert Speer, record-setting numbers of Bf 109s were produced. In total, 33,000 Bf 109s were built, more than any other aircraft. Among German aircraft, this compares with 20,000 Fw 190s and 15,000 Ju 88s. The total number of Luftwaffe aircraft of *all* types built between 1939 and 1945 was 98,755. *Bowers Collection*

The highest echelons of the German command were dragged kicking and screaming to the realization that Germany needed more fighters for *Reichsverteidigund*—

The pilots of JG 301 in 1944 and 1945 look much the same as the RAF's Battle of Britain pilots trying to relax while on alert. Now German pilots wait for the call to scramble into war-torn skies to meet the approaching enemy, in defense of the Fatherland. Night fighters could be scrambled for day or night missions. *Werner Oest*

defense of the Reich. Hitler never did fully understand or accept it. *Geschwadern* were ordered back to the Fatherland from other theaters—Italy, the Mediterranean, and Russia.

They included JG 27, JG 52, JG 53, and JG 77. In addition, some of JG 1's pilots were spun off to form the all-new JG 11 in April 1943. Supplementing the Bf 109Gs now were Focke-Wulf Fw 190s. Also on the horizon was Messerschmitt's next groundbreaking aircraft, the 262 jet fighter.

Burgeoning German fighter defenses accounted for increasing losses by the USAAF. It reached a crescendo on August 17, 1943, when the USAAF launched a mission against the Messerschmitt factory at Regensburg and ball-bearing industry at Schweinfurt. In the briefing rooms of Eighth Air Force bomber bases across East Anglia, fliers listened for their target of the day: the primary was Regensburg, with the aiming point being "the center of the Messerschmitt One Hundred and Nine G aircraft-and-engine assembly shops"—an inadvertent compliment and testimony to the threat 109s still posed in mid-1943.

Flying without fighter escort over 300 miles of enemy territory, 363 US bombers hit a wall of enemy fighters and flak, suffering 60 bombers shot down

Anything Germany could do, the United States could do more of. Here B-24 Liberators roll off the assembly line and will soon be droning over Germany from bases in England and Italy. It formed a vicious circle: The United States built strategic bombers—about 18,000 of this type alone—to destroy German war industry, and German war industry built Bf 109s to destroy them. *USAF*

and more than 100 severely damaged, most of these written off after landing. The Luftwaffe lost only 25 fighters. Beirne Lay, who later coauthored *12 O'clock High!* was flying with the low squadron of the 100th Bomb Group in a B-17 named *Piccadilly Lily*. He described how the Bf 109s "queued up like a breadline and let us have it."

"Swinging their yellow noses around in a wide U-turn, the 12-ship squadron of Me 109s came in from 12 to 2 o'clock in pairs and fours. . . . Seconds later, emergency hatches, exit doors, prematurely opened parachutes, bodies, and assorted fragments of B-17s and fighters breezed past us in the slip stream."

Proved as myth once again was the idea that bombers could protect themselves without relying on fighter escorts—the same hard lesson the Luftwaffe had learned over Great Britain. The USAAF put faith in the "combat box," a compact bomber formation in which their many guns provided shields of protective fire. With .50-caliber machine guns pointing to all directions, the firepower of a bomber formation was great, but alone not enough to overcome the advantage of enemy fighters that dove, banked, and changed speed in a heartbeat.

Between October 8 and 14, the USAAF launched more raids on war industry centers, losing another 148 bombers. Many missions saw P-38 Lightnings flying fighter escort for the greater part of the distance. But being heavier and less maneuverable, the P-38's performance could not match that of the Bf 109 and new Fw 190 interceptors. In late winter 1943, a new USAAF fighter, the P-47 Thunderbolt, assumed an escort role. It fought well, but with its large radial engine could not range much past Paris. As Knoke noted, "The Thunderbolt has a clumsy appearance which is belied by its high speed and maneuverability. It can still be outfought, however, by a Messerschmitt in the hands of a good pilot."

Allied losses in the second half of 1943 punctuated the urgent need for an effective long-range escort. That need was satisfied at the beginning of 1944, when the new P-51B Mustang swooped onto the scene. The P-51 was beyond what aircraft designers dreamed possible just a few years before, when Messerschmitts crossed the Channel, fought for 20 minutes over England, then struggled home on gasoline fumes. With a combat radius of more than 800 miles, the Mustang could escort the B-17s and B-24s all the way to their targets deep in the heart of Germany. And it was more than 30 miles per hour faster than the Bf 109, more than 20 miles per hour faster than the Fw 190. From the first day it appeared over Europe, the Rolls-Royce Merlin-powered Mustang took air combat to another level and necessitated a change of strategy for *Reichsverteidigund*.

Factory-fresh Gustavs await shuttle to first-line units. Packing the punch of two 13mm MG 131 cowl-mounted guns, a MG 151/20 or 30mm Mk. 108 cannon mounted in the engine, and two MG 151/20 underwing guns (which made it an R-6), these aircraft remained a deadly threat to Allied bombers late in the war. *Bowers Collection*

As casualties and capture wiped out Germany's veteran fighter pilots, a steady stream of new pilots flowed through flight training. With insufficient instruction, student-pilots were often sent up solo in Bf 109s with disastrous results. Many died in training. Too long in coming was the two-seat G-12 fighter-trainer, which gave better transition into the single-seat fighter. A small number were built originally at the factory as two-seaters, but most were converted Bf 109Gs relegated to training schools. *Peters Collection*

The view a Bf 109 pilot had while closing on a B-17 Flying Fortress' 6 o'clock. Bf 109s mauled the formations at every opportunity, pummeling them with machine gun and cannon shells. The bombers took enormous punishment in the skies of the Fatherland. *National Archives*

As the USAAF daylight-bombing offensive hit its stride, the RAF night bombing pounded on. Night-fighter units were elevated to a major role in defense of the Reich. The Bf 109's big brother, the Bf 110, had found good use as a night-fighter. Bf 109s also were used extensively in the role, particularly after the RAF used a new ploy called "Window." Attacking Hamburg during the night of July 24, 1943, RAF bombers had dropped "Window"—shreds of aluminum foil to confound German radar that caused mass confusion among the defenders. It allowed the RAF to slip through defenses and inflict great damage on the city. From that point on, there would not be complete reliance on radar and radio guidance for bomber detection. Fast and maneuverable Bf 109s, as well as some Fw 190s, patrolled the night skies freely at high altitudes to stalk the bombers. Called *Wilde Sau* (Wild Boar), these Bf 109s did not depend on radar; the pilot searched visually, looking for the sinister shapes of intruders against fires from burning cities and searchlights. Bf 109 pilots of the first *Nachtjagdgeschwader*, JG 300, showed incredible tenacity during the desperate months of round-the-clock bombing.

When night-fighter *Feldwebel* Richard Heemsoth's Bf 109 cannons jammed while pursuing British bombers, he resorted to desperate measures not uncommon to pilots defending the Reich. Heemsoth commented in the August 1944 issue of *Signal*:[14]

I continued firing with the machine guns, but surely with these alone I would not be able to send down this four-engined bomber. The rear gunner of the bomber must have been killed instantly because his machine guns were silent. I came a little closer, fired again until the last of my ammunition had gone. What now? I was 20 meters behind the bmber, which made the craziest turns and tried to get away in the dark. The only thing I could still do was to ram him. Slowly I came closer. It was difficult to keep the aircraft steady in his slipstream but I succeeded. My propeller crashed into the Englishman's rudder. It was a real buzz-saw. It cut through the rudder and tore it to shreds. The Englishman zoomed downward; my own machine went out of control and I was thrown out. While floating down with my parachute I lost the bomber in the darkness. Then suddenly I saw a great fire-glow down below. It had spattered with its bombs in a meadow. I came down not far away, and a quarter of an hour later I stood near the widely scattered pieces of wreckage, near a large crater in the ground . . . somewhat further away, some cows stood lowing.

Even Göring, who by now had begun to berate almost everyone and everything in his Luftwaffe, lauded the "admirable bravery of the night-fighter crews, that has brought about a new triumph over the British." Göring authorized the formation of additional *Nachtjagdgeschwadern*, JG 301 and JG 302. As the Luftwaffe regained some control over the night skies, the Wild Boars were shifted to the day-fighting role, their niche being bad weather operations.

A Last Desperate Gasp for the "Great Blow"

After the "Big Week" of mid-February 1944, when the U.S. Eighth Air Force went on a six-day bombing ram-

A wounded B-17 crewman emerges on a stretcher after the pilot nursed their bomber home to Bury St. Edmunds in eastern England. *94th BGMA*

Despite Hitler's ranting that bombers must remain the highest priority, fighter production hit a peak of 2,500 in September 1944, according to Adolf Galland.

Now, aircraft numbers were no longer the problem. *Fuel* was. Through missions of the U.S. 15th Air Force, newly based in the Mediterranean, the Allies wisely focused on destruction of the German petroleum industry, particularly the oil fields of German satellite Romania. While production numbers for both Bf 109s and Fw 190s grew, production of aviation fuel dropped inversely: 195,000 tons of fuel in May 1944, 35,000 tons in July, falling to a trickle of 7,000 tons in September.

page on concentrated industry centers, *Reichsminister* Albert Speer dispersed German war industry. In the reorganization and reprioritization that followed, he gave priority to fighter production, increasing totals from 900 new fighters in the month of February to some 2,000 in

Another factor det-rimental to fighter forces was the diminishing quality of pilots. Many of the great veterans were gone. Men like Marseille died over Africa; Wolfgang Schellmann was executed as a Russian prisoner; Werner Mölders died while flying as a passenger; appalling numbers of top-flight Bf 109 pilots had died in the frigid waters of the North Sea during the Battle of Britain and in the expansive sky of Russia. While the Luftwaffe training command was pumping out pilots by the hundreds, the graduates lacked proper training and experience, logging barely half the flight time of pilot-students before the war. As Galland noted, "In August 1,000 fighter pilots left the schools. Their standard was by no means satisfactory and their training needed an additional 15 flying hours . . .. The American observation that our pilots showed 'more fighting spirit than ability' was sad but true." Lack of fuel also compounded the training problem, precious little being left for training as front-line units faced life-and-death battles daily.

A dramatic intervention was needed. Fighter chief General Galland grasped at one of few logical alternatives open to him: Rather than use up the fuel drop by drop as soon as it came, he would conserve his resources, store up fuel, fully outfit all operational units with the abundance of aircraft—and launch an all-out operation against the Allied air forces. Even though losses would be unspeakable, likely costing him a third of his fighter force, it might stem the overwhelming tide of bombers,

If B-17s made it through the gauntlet of German fighters and flak, they often returned to base riddled with holes. *National Archives and 94th BGMA*

as it had done temporarily in the second half of 1943.

Galland explained:

> My main desire was to create a new reserve . . . Oddly enough, my proposal to give priority to the replenishing and formation of reserves instead of sending forces to the front was accepted without demur by the Supreme Command. As on my two previous attempts in this direction, I maintained that this was the only possible way to deliver the necessary "great blow" in the defense of the Reich. The "great blow" became the slogan. It seemed that wings had been given to all who worked for the reconstruction of the fighter arm in the hope of meeting the enemy once more with some decisive chance of success. It should have been possible to reverse things in the air at home with about 2,000 to 3,000 fighter planes and this was our aim. . . .

As summer and fall 1944 dragged on, the Luftwaffe slowly gained strength through conservation. But things would not go as Galland planned. After the June 6 Normandy invasion, the Allied ground forces were moving steadily east toward Germany. In December 1944, Hitler made a last, desperate lunge with an offensive in the Ardennes region of Belgium, known as the Battle of the Bulge.

Just before Galland could launch the "great blow," Göring diverted the fighter forces in support of the offensive. His plan was to throw the *Jagdgeschwadern* at the forward Allied airfields in Belgium, France, and the Netherlands. Bf 109G-10s, G-14s, and K-4s, mixed within *Gruppen*, would see action. Bf 109 units diverted for Operation *Bodenplatte* were JG 1, JG 2, JG 3, JG 4, JG 6, JG 11, JG 26, JG 27, JG 53, and JG 77.

On New Year's Day 1945, a surprise attack by 900 German planes targeted Allied airfields in Belgium, France, and the Netherlands. A profusion of Mustangs, Thunderbolts, and Spitfires scrambled. The attack cost the Luftwaffe 300 aircraft, about half of them Bf 109s, and destroyed only about 200 Allied aircraft. The Bf 109s and other aircraft were easily replaceable, but the pilots weren't. Only about a fifth of them lived to fight another day, and the rest were killed or captured.

The day had marked the start of a new year and the end of major Bf 109 operations. The mission accomplished little and was ruinous to the Luftwaffe. The last major German offensive stalled by mid-January.

After this, there were intermittent air battles, fought desperately and without hope for victory. For example, on April 7, 1945, 120 Bf 109Gs intercepted large formations of USAAF bombers. The pilots, mostly students with minimal flight hours and no combat experience, were ordered to ram the bombers if they had to. Of those 120 Bf 109s, only 15 survived.

The *Jagdgeschwadern*, once the scourge of European skies, were no more. Soldiering right up to the end, the Bf 109 had the most incredible combat record of any aircraft ever built. In a world where the number of air victories meant everything, no aircraft was more victorious than the Bf 109: According to *The Luftwaffe War Diaries*, 103 fighter pilots reached the 100 mark for victories; 13 reached 200; and two pilots reached 300. Eric Hartmann scored his 352nd victory just hours before the end of hostilities in May 1945, when he downed a Yak 11. That is the highest number, for all nations, in all wars, and likely the highest there will ever be. He flew Bf 109s exclusively. Second-highest was Gerhard Barkhorn with 301 victories. And Günther Rall scored 275, despite severe injuries from crashes that grounded him for months.

The Bf 109 was the deadly instrument in a losing cause, a heinously evil cause, but its successes as a fighter aircraft are indisputable.

Smoke pours from this Bf 109 in a rapid-frame succession that shows first the canopy fluttering upward as the pilot begins a tumbling descent. The victor's gun camera remains trained on the aircraft. Out of the frame, the pilot succeeded in deploying his parachute, according to the official USAF caption. Then the aircraft exploded. *USAF via Ethell*

CHAPTER 9

PILOT TALK: BRITISH & AMERICAN

THE FOLLOWING PILOT RECOUNTS ARE EXCERPTS FROM OTHER PUBLICATIONS (AS NOTED) AND DIRECT QUOTES FROM INTERVIEWS.

Jeffrey Quill: British Test Pilot

"In October 1940 I flew a captured Me 109E; to my surprise and relief I found the aileron control of the German fighter at high speed every bit as bad as, if not worse than, the Spitfire I and II with fabric-covered ailerons. It was good at low and medium speed, but at 400 miles per hour and above it was almost immovable. I thought the Me 109E performed well, particularly on the climb at altitude, and it had good stalling characteristics under G, except that the leading-edge slats kept snapping in and out. It had no rudder trimmer, which gave it a heavy footload at high speed, while the cockpit, the canopy and the rearward vision were much worse than in the Spitfire.

The A & AEE reported on the Me 109E in October 1941: "The flying controls have excellent response and feel at low speeds but are far too heavy for maneuvering at high speeds. The extreme heaviness of the ailerons makes rolling almost impossible at speeds above 400 miles per hour." So we were not the only ones in trouble in 1940. . .

The first time I sighted Me 109s in the air we had been vectored out over the Channel toward a formation of "bandits," which was alleged to be coming in roughly the opposite direction. I was flying in the fourth section, to the rear of the squadron, when I was aware of black smoke coming from the exhausts of our leading aircraft as Sam Saunders had started climbing furiously and turning left-handed.

As a Supermarine test pilot, Jeffrey Quill tested Spitfires and also flew them against Bf 109s. The elliptical-winged Spitfire was designed by Reginald Mitchell, well known from his designs for the world-record-holding Schneider Cup racing seaplanes. The Spitfire flew for the first time on March 5, 1936, and when the last one rolled off the line in 1947, a total of 20,351 had been built. *National Archives*

Then I saw them, about 1,000 feet higher than we were, over to our left, and in a fairly tight formation . . . about 20, I estimated. They looked like silvery minnows with their down-swept noses, and I could see the black crosses on their fuselages. Then they started to swing round in a diving turn toward us. They had the advantage of speed and height, so we continued climbing and turning furiously. To my astonishment the 109s, having turned left-handed through 180 degrees, dived away toward the French coast without making the slightest attempt to attack us. We immediately gave chase, but only our leading few aircraft were close enough to open fire. I could see the tracer trails and was mightily impressed by the bullet drop thus displayed, at once realizing why one needed to get close to get a hit. . . . Sam Saunders called off the chase—very properly, because the 109s, losing height rapidly as they were, could well have been leading us into a trap.

One engagement with several Me 109s at about 25,000 feet over the Channel happened very suddenly. I found myself behind two 109s in a steep left-hand turn. I was able to turn inside the second one and fired at him from close range. He went on pulling round as sharply as he could and I followed him without any difficulty and went on firing bursts at him and saw puffs of black smoke and then a trail of white vapor streaming from him. By this time I could no longer see the first 109 and then realized he was on my tail. As I was by now just shuddering on the G stall, I quickly turned inward and dived. I pulled up again when I was sure I had shaken him off and, as usual on these occasions, found myself apparently completely alone in the sky and thoroughly disoriented with wildly spinning compass and gyro instruments. I was pleased with that little episode, partly because I was damn sure that the first 109 was not going to get home and, secondly, because I was now absolutely sure the Spitfire Mk. I could readily out-turn the 109, certainly in the 20,000 feet area. . . ."

(Excerpt from *Spitfire: A Test Pilot's Story* by Jeffrey Quill. Crécy Publishing Limited © 1998.)

Jack Ilfrey: P-38 and P-51 Pilot, 20th Fighter Group, USAAF

The first time I encountered a 109 was December 2, 1942. I was with the 94th "Hat in the Ring" Squadron, 1st Fighter Group, flying P-38s out of a makeshift field in North Africa called Youks-les-Bains. Here we came up against some of Rommel's topnotch Luftwaffe pilots.

It was only our second mission[16] and four of us were supposed to attack gun emplacements and pillboxes at Faid Pass, in the mountains near Kasserine Pass. At 7:30 A.M., we strafed the ground targets and flew to the Mediterranean coast, where we strafed a German or Italian ship in the harbor at Sfax. Then we headed south along the coast to Gabes, close to the southern Tunisian border and Libya.

We were pretty low, around 500 or 600 feet as we came up on Gabes. Behind the town we could see that

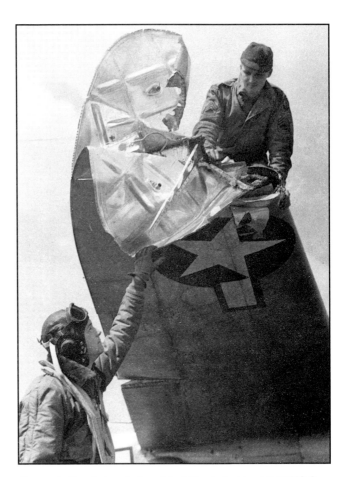

Damage to the starboard wing of Jack Ilfrey's Lockheed P-38 MC-0, after a collision with a Bf 109 over Berlin on May 24, 1944. Ilfrey was able to nurse the big fighter home, but the Bf 109 went down—earning Ilfrey his fourth victory over a Bf 109. *Jack Ilfrey*

there was a dirt airfield with a lot of equipment on it—planes, tanks, and supplies.

The flight leader suddenly yelled on the radio: "Four bandits taking off. I'll take the first one." The four bandits were Messerschmitt 109s. Four of them and four us. Pretty evenly matched, except that we had a big advantage of altitude and speed. It was pretty easy for him to get the first one as it took off. His wingman got the second one. I followed and went after the third, as did my wingman after the fourth.

The third one was leaving the ground and had just got his wheels up. As he began to bank, I took aim and pushed the button, causing four .50-caliber machine guns and one 20mm cannon to spurt several hundred rounds. He seemed to stay in that bank for a long time, then his wingtip hit the ground and he cartwheeled and exploded.

This was only the second time I had fired in anger. All this came off pretty good. But I made the mistake of turning around and going back over the field. Alone. We had gotten separated and the flight leader had not called us back together.

Taking off right in front of me was another 109. He came at me head-on and firing—about 400 feet off the ground. What my eyes fixated on was the big old orange ball coming from the cannon in his nose. The P-38 was the best gun platform of any fighter I knew, with guns in the nose like the 109's cannon, letting you aim right on your axis. I started firing, too, as we whizzed past each other.

He was hit. I was hit, too. The strikes sounded like hail on a tin roof. I turned in time to see a line of bullets marching up my left nacelle tearing up the skin. He also put a shell into my right engine, severed an oil line and froze it up. I got right down on the deck and feathered the prop.

Meantime, there were several other Me 109s taking off. My flight was trying to get back together. But I was still down on the deck. Two more 109s had taken off and started chasing me. On one engine I could only do about 250 or 260. Both made a pass on me trying to knock me down. Finally, my flight leader came over to help, only to discover he was out of ammunition. But the other two boys had also heard me and closed in.

One of my fellows radioed, "Weave, Jack, weave." So I was weaving in and out of sand dunes as the 109s were firing at me. The closer you got to the ground, the harder it was for them to get you. The two wingmen shot down one 109 and chased away the other. Otherwise I would never have made it back 60 miles back to Youks-les-Bains.

Then-Captain Jack Ilfrey. *Jack Ilfrey*

In April 1943, I had completed my tour and I was down somewhere around Casa Blanca waiting for a ride home. Several captured German planes had been sent here to this depot. I noticed that they had this Me 109.

I got to talking with some of the sergeants who were working on it. First they said they had inspected it thoroughly for booby traps. Then they started working on the engine and different things. One said to me, "It purrs like a kitten." And a couple others said, "Why don't you take it out?" A master sergeant came out while I was standing there. He could speak German and was reading the instrument panel, telling me this was this and that was that.

Then the master sergeant grabbed a roll of adhesive tape like used for bandages and wrote names in English for all the instruments and taped over the German words. Gas tank, air speed, carburetor controls, and the throttle controls.

I climbed in and found the cockpit was cramped. I was only 145 pounds, and 5 feet 10 inches tall, but it was tight as I strapped in. Then off I went.

My first thought was: *This is a mean little beast.* To start with, in a P-38 you had complete straight-ahead visibility. In the 109 you had to slither like a snake when you taxied because you couldn't see straight ahead. And we knew that a lot of the German pilots had ground looped them.

The P-38 was so smooth on takeoff. In both the 109 and Mustang, you had torque to fool with. It was very similar to a P-51 at takeoff. My reaction as I lifted was: *Good goddam, it works!*

I did some acrobatics over the field and watched American soldiers running for cover all over the place. (The aircraft was still painted in the Luftwaffe colors.) I kind of got a kick out of that. I don't think anyone was hurt, but I caught the devil for it later.

Germans used the metric system—kilometers per hour. Since we used miles per hour, I didn't know how fast I was going. I had to fly based strictly on feel.

I found the one thing the master sergeant hadn't marked was the flaps. He had marked the landing gear, but not the flaps. I hadn't thought of it either. I saw what looked like should have been the flaps, but I didn't want to pull on it not knowing what it might be. The area was like a dry lake, nice and wide open, kind of like what's near Edwards Air Force Base. So there was lots of maneuvering room, but I had to come in without flaps. That made speed higher. I had a hell of a time making it stay on the ground. But I was never in any danger of ground looping, and I stopped safely.

I got in trouble right away when I climbed out of the cockpit. The general commanding the 9th Air Force made it clear this little flight was *not* the thing to do. (Being one of America's first aces, however, no doubt excused a lot at the time!)

The next victory over a 109 was May 24, 1944. We were up above 30,000 feet, higher than the bombers. We were the first fighter group to get near Berlin. The sky was full of the bombers and fighters. Americans and Germans all around each other. Kind of like mayhem. I thought to myself, *What in the hell is all this—everyone up here trying to kill one another?*

We spotted a gaggle of 109s—we called 'em gaggles—30 or 40 109s coming down on us. Their idea was to get us out of the way so that they could shoot down the bombers. When they went through we got scattered like a swarm of bees. I ended up pointed directly toward a 109 coming head on.

I fired and hit him, but just after I'd shot down this one someone broke radio silence. The voice says, "Jack, there's one coming up underneath you!" I dipped my wing to look down, because I couldn't see directly down. That instant I felt a jolt, and caught a glimpse of my right wing slicing right across the cockpit of a 109. It wasn't really a feeling of shock, it was more like just "Oh, shit."

I didn't have time to watch what happened to him. The collision knocked off about 3 feet of my right wing. I had been feeding on my right outer wing tank. When we hit, it ruptured that tank, so all the gas came running out and the engine quit. A little bit of fire, but not much because we were at such high altitude.

The collision damage threw my P-38 into a spin. I was seeing aircraft everywhere I turned—and what seemed like hundreds of parachutes coming out of bombers and fighters. (But no parachute out of this German fighter, as other pilots later told Ilfrey.) A spin was easily correctable in a P-38, but I thought to myself, *Here I am on one engine—and they're all around me.* So I made a split-second decision to let my P-38 stay in that spin so I could duck down into a layer of clouds, at about 16,000 to 18,000 feet. Then I straightened myself out and switched gas tanks. While in the clouds, I was able to get my right engine running.

From southeast of Berlin, I made it the 500 miles back to England. Once on the ground, I looked underneath at the damage on my plane to see if that 109 had been firing as he was coming up to me. Didn't find any holes. It's possible that with all the twisting and turning we were doing that he didn't see me until the last second and didn't have time to open fire.

The American pilot who'd radioed me told me later he was sure we'd collide and both of us would be nothing but bits and pieces. He didn't know if the collision decapitated the 109 pilot, but it certainly killed him. He saw the 109 nose down and fly directly into the ground. After all this was reported to intelligence, I got credit for it.

Douglas Bader:
Spitfire and Hurricane Pilot, RAF

The Luftwaffe started the war equipped with a good fighter, the Me 109, which was used throughout the war. It had two major disadvantages. First, it was not as strong as the British fighters and therefore the German pilots could not dive it as fast or for as long as we could with ours. (One of their top fighter pilots, Baltazar, had died when the wings of his Me 109 folded up on him in a dive. It happened to other German pilots too, which was bad for morale.) Secondly, the petrol tank was L-shaped and fitted around the pilot's seat. This was highly vulnerable to attack, even though it was covered with armor plate.

We British fighter pilots could not know all these murky details about the 109 until afterward. But during the Battle of Britain, we soon discovered that the 109 pilots would not hold the dive and pulled out slowly. There was another significant difference between the Me 109 and the two British fighters. All three airplanes were powered by liquid-cooled V-12 engines. The Rolls-Royce Merlin sat upright in the Hurricane and Spitfire and was normally aspirated with a carburetor. But the Daimler-Benz in the Me 109 was inverted and used petrol injection. The normal escape method of a Me 109 pilot with a British fighter on his tail was to push the stick forward and go straight into a steep dive. With petrol injection the negative 'G' caused by this maneuver did not affect his engine. When the Spitfire or Hurricane pilot tried to follow, the reverse pressure impeded the flow of petrol through the carburetor of his Rolls-Royce Merlin and the engine stopped instantly. The infuriating result was that by the time you came over the top and your engine had picked up, the Me 109 was thousands of feet below, if indeed you ever saw him again.

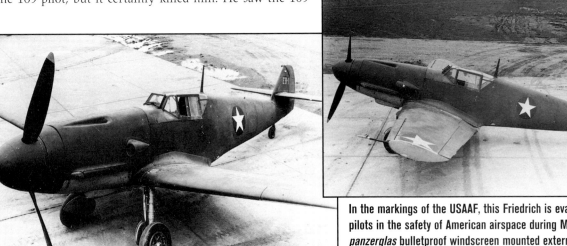

In the markings of the USAAF, this Friedrich is evaluated by American pilots in the safety of American airspace during May 1942. It has a *panzerglas* bulletproof windscreen mounted externally. Note the automatic wing slots slid forward. *National Archives*

We used to discuss this problem among ourselves, to see if we could work out some method of getting at the 109 before we lost him. The method we evolved was to half-roll to start the dive thus keeping the engine going but turning our back on the Me 109; then an aileron turn to restore direction and hope to see the enemy once more. Surprisingly, this seemingly complicated idea worked quite well in practice.

Once we discovered how to stay with the Me 109 at the beginning of its dive, its structural weakness became evident. The Me 109 pilot of those days would dive away at about 75 degrees (not quite vertical) but he would never hold the dive for long. On such an occasion a 109 left my Hurricane standing in the initial stage of the dive, but he started pulling out gently long before I expected and I overhauled him. My maximum airspeed on the clock, at 8,000 feet where I started to pull out, was only 320 miles per hour and yet I was closing the gap quickly. I remember the occasion as though it were yesterday. The Hurricane was bigger, slower, and less streamlined than the Messerschmitt or the Spitfire. It appeared impossible to catch the former in a dive, but other Hurricane pilots had similar experiences to mine. The advantage of the Spitfire and the Hurricane in individual combat with a Me 109 was that both British airplanes could out-turn the German one which was why, when surprised from behind, the enemy's defensive maneuver was to push the stick forward into a dive which, in 1940, we could not follow. If we were surprised, our defense was to turn quickly and keep turning because the Me 109's radius of turn was bigger than that of the Spitfire or Hurricane and thus he could not keep you in his sights. If he was inexperienced enough to try, he would find the British fighter behind him after a couple of circuits.

Nevertheless, the Me 109 was a good fighter airplane. It was smaller than its British counterparts, faster than the Hurricane, and about the same in speed and climb as the Spitfire. At first it carried mixed armament consisting of two 15mm cannons and two machine guns. Later models from the F range onward had what some of us regarded as the best idea of all—a cannon firing through the center of the propeller spinner. This was a brilliant innovation since, unlike having guns in the wings, the attitude of the airplane did not matter." (Excerpt from *Fight for the Sky: The Story of the Spitfire and Hurricane* by Douglas Bader. Sidgwick & Jackson. © 1990.)

Dennis Sherman: Modern-Day Warbird Pilot and Owner of a Spanish-Built Bf 109 (HA-1112-M1L)

I started flying as a kid, and flew midget racers and homebuilts and warbirds, so I have a lot of experience in a lot of different airplanes. I had never flown a 109 and I knew it was a very rare airplane. And a difficult one. I've owned at least half a dozen Mustangs. Corsairs, too. Also, a Hellcat, Lightning, Kingcobra, and Skyraider.

For a World War II fighter, the 109 is the smallest of all of them. It has a menacing look about it. It's a mean-looking little airplane—made more so by the swastika and black crosses. When people walked up casually to look it over, the first thing they'd comment on was the unusual landing gear. They'd look at that and laugh.

The one thing I thought about as I approached the 109 for the first time was the terrible reputation that it had and how I didn't want to add to that reputation. The worst part of it was *thinking about flying it*, before you even fired up the motor. Once you got in, you were concentrating on not tearing it up. The cockpit is small and quite blind. Compared to the other World War II fighters I've owned, none come close to being that small. And it has a very small windshield.

The Bearcat is also nice and small. But unlike the 109, the Bearcat has a huge bubble canopy that offers excellent visibility. When you sit in either of those airplanes your shoulders just about touch the sides. I say *nice* and small, because I like that—you really felt like part of the airplane once you're in it. But getting strapped is a pain, because it's so confining. You feel that even more when you close the heavy canopy hinged on the side of the 109. When you close it, you can see hardly a thing on the ground.

This Bf 109G-5 or G-6 (in natural aluminum finish) has been modified in postwar. Photographed on October 5, 1945, the aircraft is minus cowl guns, and the landing gear legs appear shortened. Paint has been stripped and inaccurate wartime German markings have been reapplied.
National Archives

Before start-up you make sure that the radiators are in the open position. This aircraft has a manual primer on it and electric boost pumps. It has great big slide-type key for the magnetos. And a booster coil. After priming it, you turn the boost pump on and start spinning it over. At the same time, you hold the booster coil and turn the mags on. This one started easily. Once it started, the whole airplane would shake. The wings would rock up and down. And the spinning propeller looked huge on this little tiny airplane.

Unfortunately, you could not taxi with the canopy open. Probably the worst airplane to taxi ever. Plus, the first time I tried to taxi, I found that this very strong centering tail-wheel made the airplane just want to go straight. When I taxi an airplane, I like to be smooth with it. With the 109, I found myself pushing real hard on the brake, but it just kept going straight. I had the boys on the wingtips trying to help me. Finally, I just decided the only way you could make the damn thing turn was to jab the power on and push the stick full forward to lighten the tail and get it rolling, then stomp on the brake real hard and it would turn about 10 degrees. The tail-wheel would kick out and let you turn, but then it would go back into lock mode.

So it was kind of like a drunken sailor trying to taxi the thing. A lot of weight on the tail, probably built that way for the fields they typically flew out of. Unlike the Spitfire, it would be very hard to nose over. Once you're lined up with the runway, you set the radiators—close them up to about half position. And you go to zero boost, which is 30 inches of manifold pressure, and then you just ease the power up.

On my first takeoff, I took off with the flaps up. The airplane with the flaps up feels like a much higher wing loading than with the flaps down. The airplane is a lot more buoyant when you do use flaps in takeoff. It gets into the air much quicker. And it makes the wing loading appear to be lighter, which it really isn't. But that way you had that extra lift.

I never had any problems running out of rudder, and it's an extremely small rudder. You can't believe that this tiny airplane with its tiny rudder and big engine has so much rudder authority, but it does. You could pour on the power for takeoff. A lot people said not to, but after we flew it for a while we found that we were getting on it hard and that was the fun of takeoff in the 109.

Once in the air, the gear came up very, very fast. Then you start cranking up the flaps. Then just reduce power. It had a boost gauge rather than a manifold pressure gauge, and our redline was about 14 inches of boost—about 58 inches. Normally we used about 12, or about 54 inches of pressure.

From entries in my logbook, I see that at 2,300 rpm and 34 inches at 11,000 feet, it indicated 200 knots and true airspeed at 245 knots with the temperature that day. Then

Dennis Sherman and his sons made between 140 and 150 flights in this Spanish-built version of the Bf 109, the HA-1112-M1L, painted in German markings and the wartime mottled paint scheme. The aircraft is now at the Cavanaugh Air Museum in Addison, Texas. *EAA/Jim Koepnick*

I ran it at 12,000 feet at 2,400 rpm and 38 inches, and it indicated 220 knots and trued out to 315 miles per hour.

The aircraft feels good. Feels solid.

There is no rudder trim. So to keep the ball center, you had to hold rudder. But the rudder pressure is very light. In the air, it was smooth. There was a harmonic area in our aircraft around 2,600 rpm. But you just avoid that, or go through that area quickly.

As you slow up, the leading edge slats start creeping out. Unless you look at them, you might not realize they are even working. But they work very nicely. Stall characteristics were great. With the gear out, slats out, and full flaps, it would stall indicate at about 75 knots. Good compared to many other World War II fighters.

The trim wheel and the flap wheel are side by side on the left side of the airplane. They're two big wheels that let you use your hand to turn the flaps and trim at the same time. The trim wheel actually moves the whole horizontal stabilizer up and down. In flight, the first 10 degrees of flap is quite easy. When you wanted full flaps, you had to pull quite hard, because there was a lot more drag.

Other flight characteristics: It had a nice roll rate. Ailerons were fairly light. Elevators were very heavy. Unlike a Mustang, which, of course, is a much more modern airplane, the 109 really seems to slow up when you got to 275 to 300 knots indicated. A Mustang seems to keep going.

I looped it, rolled it, and stalled it. When you drop down to about 50 feet off the ground, I would always trim the horizontal stabilizer completely nose up, to make the tail go down. When you head down to land, the landing gear comes out very quickly. *Clunk, clunk.* You can really feel it when it comes out. Then you start to slowing up and trimming the flaps and the elevator trim together. I always made a high turning approach, so I could see out of that canopy.

You had to get the airplane on short final slow enough so the slats would come out. With the slats out, the nose of the airplane has a tendency to be at a level attitude, so your forward visibility was nil because of the attitude. If you came in too fast, too close to the ground, and then tried to slow up, the slats would come out and give you more lift, which only aggravated the situation. The secret was to get it slowed up enough so the slats were out, then you could use your throttle to help regulate your rate of descent.

We would always try to three-point. Sometimes it was easy, sometimes not. It seemed like it would always stall before the tail-wheel would get on the ground. The landing never really felt like screechers. I would watch my two sons land it, and I would tell them, "That looked like a good landing." And they would say, "Not from where I was sitting."

The 109 has a reputation for ground looping. A more likely time to ground loop is when a plane is slowing up, at low speeds. In the 109, I never saw that happen. It would make a dart *early* in the landing roll, not at the end of the landing roll.

The closest call I had on landing was when I had to land with a strong crosswind, at almost precisely 90 degrees. I touched down and was still rolling pretty fast. There happened to be a big dip in the grass runway, and it launched me back up in the air again. I had absolutely no control, so I was just hanging on. Anyhow, it came back down and I didn't tear it up.

We had heard about overheating problems with this type of aircraft, considering the fact that the radiators were actually outboard of the prop arc. But we never had that problem. Ours cooled extremely well. I think part of the secret was not to do a hard run-up before takeoff. In other words, if you were just idling and taxiing, it was all right. If you had to sit there and run up and got the temperature run up, and you had to sit there more, there might have been overheating problems. If we did have to idle, we'd turn the nose into the wind and let it idle. But that was a difference from the Mustang, which you simply point into the wind and run at 1,500 rpm to cool it because the radiator is right in the prop wash.

The first day that we all flew it, we were pleasantly surprised to find that, especially on grass, it didn't really have the terrible tendencies that we had heard so much about. However, the airplane is such that, some days, you think it's a piece of cake. And the next time, you think, *Wow, this really got my attention.* The biggest thing is the landing gear. The struts, when they get weight on them, especially if one strut gets weight on before the other one, tends to change the gear geometry and darts.

When I was flying off of concrete, which eventually we did most all the time, it would seem that when you touched down it would roll pretty straight for about the first 200 feet, then all of a sudden it would take a violent dart one way or the other. When it would do that you would just jam on the full opposite rudder and hit the brake. After about two or three sashays like that, you'd be down to 60 or 70 knots. Then it would feel like it was on

rails, going straight as could be. It was like it had said, "Okay, you're awake. Now I'm going to leave you alone."

Looking in my logbook, I see I made a total of 45 flights in the 109. My two sons also flew the airplane, about the same number of flights. They had more hours in it because they took it places. My oldest son flew it to several airshows, to Oshkosh (Wisconsin), and to Texas. I just enjoyed going up and down, and doing aerobatics in it. There were close to 140 to 150 flights between the three of us.

Dr. Bill Harrison: Modern-Day Warbird Pilot and Owner of a Spanish-Built Bf 109 (HA-1112-M1L)

When you look at a 109, it looks like a weapon of war. That's what it's designed for, that's what it does. It's a very fundamental airplane.

You have to think about that it was a 1930s fighter, not a 1940s fighter. The canopy is multibeveled instead of bubble. Visibility is really pretty poor. It has a very cramped cockpit. Very, very narrow landing gear. But it was a good attack plane—a cannon in the nose and pretty good firepower. They put in a bulletproof windshield and an armor plate behind the pilot's head, so survivability was pretty good.

To taxi it, you have to S-turn, so you're constantly looking out the side. You look down the left side then you turn to the left, so that you go the direction you've been looking; you look to the right side and then turn to the right. You never *ever* see in front of you. A lot of planes are like that, including the Corsair and Mustang, although not quite as bad as the 109. In the Corsair and Mustang, the canopy is bubbled enough that you can lean over and see a little bit, but in the 109 there is just that flat side. There's no easy way to do it. You have to roll on the ground and depend on "impressions."

You really sat on the gas tank. The gas tank was shaped like a shoe and you sat on the toe of it and leaned on the back of it. The gas tank really makes the seat.

This aircraft had the Merlin engine. The Daimler-Benz, since it was an inverted V, gave a different thrust line. The propeller line with the Daimler was different and the visibility was better, because the nose was a little lower. Apparently that also affected the way it flew.

The World War II German pilots I've talked with loved it in combat, because it did exactly what it was supposed to do. While I owned it, I never had a World War II German pilot ask me to fly it for old times' sake—I guess people who flew it in combat didn't care to fly it again for pleasure. One told me, "I used to fly the 109, but most of the time I flew the 190 because I wasn't strong enough."

It was a very heavy airplane on the controls, and it took a lot of strength to fly it, even though it was a little airplane. The 109 has no boost on any of the controls. I don't mean hydraulic, but dynamic boost. No servo boost.

110

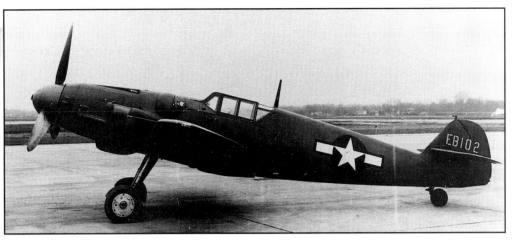

This Bf 109G/Trop carries standard U.S. wartime markings and EB102 on its tail, ready for testing at Wright Field, Dayton, Ohio. By the time this aircraft would have reached American hands (photographed on February 28, 1944), it seems unlikely much could be learned from testing the outmoded Messerschmitt to enhance American fighters. *National Archives*

There were no gap seals in the ailerons. So as the airspeed increases, the turbulence increases and it sort of locks the controls. Very, very stiff. I could roll it to the left pretty well because I'm right-handed. And my strength is pushing to the left. But to the right, when I was going over 300 knots, it was just impossible for me to make it roll. It took both hands.

If you watch some of the old World War II film, most of the attacks are diving, rolling attacks—to the left.

It's a very light airplane for the power it has. So the power-to-weight ratio is superb. On the ground, if you can keep it going straight, you'll be in the air very quickly. And it'll climb quite well. I didn't ever get a chance to fly it on grass, which I wanted to do.

It does have some interesting flight characteristics: It has a very long tail. A long moment arm on the elevator. So the stick pressures are light, in terms of elevator, which is in direct contrast to the ailerons that, like I've said, are very stiff. One problem with this is it will change the way the airplane is *pointed*, but it won't change the way the airplane is *going*. Because it has so little wing that the mass really tends to continue moving the same direction. The Russian Yak also doesn't have much wing, so it's similar to the 109 in that it continues to fly even though you change the pointing direction. A Corsair, in comparison, flies on its wing so it doesn't tend to do that.

The 109's slats were quite an innovation at the time. It really improved the low-speed handling of the airplane. The problem with it is that they have to deploy at the same time or you have a problem. Not an insurmountable problem, but a problem. One of the tests (in preflight) is to take one finger and push on either end of the slat and it should go up and back without any binding.

It does get interesting if one slat comes out asymmetrically. People I've talked with suggest that on landing, you slow it down fairly high to get the slats out, because you really don't want them coming out right at touchdown. So you slow it down up higher than you might do with other fighters.

The French Rallye airplane also had these slats that are air-activated, like the 109. In that plane, one slat did stick during a flight. It was controllable, but as it gets slower it gets harder because you have to land it a little faster.

Slats or no slats, the 109 was a challenge to land. I tore up my 109 landing. I had been down to do the Confederate Air Force show when it had been in Harlingen (Texas). I was coming home to Tulsa when I decided to stop and spend the night with my parents in Waco, Texas, where I grew up. So I landed there and left it at the airport there overnight. When I went out there the next morning to leave, I found a few drops of hydraulic fluid underneath, but there was plenty in the reservoir so I didn't worry about it.

I took off and hit the gear lever and the gear came up about halfway and quit. It wouldn't come up all the way.

When you want to land, the gear will free fall, so it wasn't a big worry. But I thought about flying on to Tulsa with the gear down, and decided that it was kind of silly. I decided to land to see what was wrong. That was probably mistake number one, because I still had a full fuel tank. And the fuel . . . like I said, you're sitting on it. So that puts you about four feet aft of the center of lift—very tail heavy. That's not a good place to be. And because of that, I decided I would land it on the wheels instead of three-pointing it.

I got it down on the wheels. Everything was going straight. The wind was going down the runway. No major complicating factors at that point. But I started to put the brakes on and the left brake locked on and found I had no right brake. So at about 75 or 80 knots, the airplane snapped 90 degrees sideways. One gear went one way and the other gear went the other way. Both wings broke off and the fuselage broke in the middle.

When they disassembled the airplane back in England to rebuild it, they found that the reason for all this was that a cotter pin had been left out of the brake assembly.

When I had it, it was painted in the North African paint scheme. It was rebuilt, torn up again, and rebuilt again, this time redone in a Continental Europe paint scheme. (This same aircraft, later owned by Dennis Sherman, is now in Cavanaugh Flight Museum, Addison, Texas.)

CHAPTER 10

TWILIGHT YEARS

Service After the Luftwaffe

When Field Marshal Alfred Jodl signed Germany's surrender in the wee hours of May 7, 1945, hundreds of Bf 109s stood mute and spectral on bomb-cratered airfields across Europe. Many were virtually brand new and intact, with flight hours equal only to ferrying time from the factory—testimony to Speer's persevering production, and lack of fuel and pilots to fly them.

Assembly lines widely dispersed in the face of massive Allied bombing had continued producing Bf 109s right up to the end. Some of the subcontractor and assembly facilities, like those in Prague, were located away from the fighting and bombing, and they remained largely unscathed. These now stood mute, too, with rows of unfinished airframes amidst the punches, dies, jigs, and engineering drawings that created them.

Almost none of the Bf 109s parked at that moment on German airfields, far-flung fields in Norway, or the Courland pocket in Latvia would survive the massive scrapping program instituted after the surrender. The victorious Allies marching into Germany naturally wanted its foe completely disarmed. They also wanted some reclamation of the vast materials stolen to make the Nazi war machine. The scrapping was executed immediately and with astonishing thoroughness, considering the huge numbers.

Several Bf 109 fuselages and remnants of various other German aircraft litter a one-time civilian airport near Hangelar. Surveying the wreckage is a soldier from the 78th Division, 1st U.S. Army. Number 8 has smashed glass but its Erla Haube canopy's frame is intact. Hangelar is located on the Rhine River's east bank, opposite Bonn. *National Archives*

Only a handful of Bf 109s built in time for wartime service, along with select other German combat aircraft like the Messerschmitt 262, were hand-picked by U.S. and British researchers for testing. These were brought back to Wright Field at Dayton, Ohio, and the RAE at Farnborough, England. Some of those few test specimens survived in museums or were restored in later years. The rest went to the smelters throughout Europe.

And that was the end of the Messerschmitt Bf 109 story. Or was it?

As it turns out, despite the end of hostilities, despite the advent of the "Jet Age" led by Messerschmitt's own 262, and despite the Bf 109's obsolescence compared to even other propeller-powered fighters, *it wasn't*.

Mass disposal was a great dismay to certain small countries. Digging out of the rubble of World War II, many countries were desperate to reestablish military defenses. They did not view the surviving Bf 109s as scrap iron. They viewed the aircraft as a prime choice for the home-defense role, because of its simplicity, proven effectiveness, and relatively low cost. Only two Luftwaffe combat aircraft types saw postwar military service: the Bf 109 and Heinkel He 111.

Through a gathering of remnants—partially built airframes, subcontractor materials, incomplete engineering plans—and the small number of aircraft exported by

Several Bf 109s, including probable K or late G versions, stand amidst protective earth-mound revetments. Their almost certain fate is the smelter. *Bowers Collection*

Germany during the war, the Bf 109 (in various forms) would remain in production and on active duty in countries around the world for years to come.

Czechoslovakia

The Avia factory at Prague-Cakovice was a contributor to Speer's dispersed war industry. As a final assembly facility for the Bf 109, it was the centerpiece of Prague's many small subcontracting factories that manufactured various aircraft components.

On the assembly line at the time the Russians marched through Czechoslovakia were Bf 109G-14s. These were among the first to be built at the newly established site. In the panic of the retreat, the Germans left the Avia facility operational. And even more remarkable, the Soviet juggernaut stomping on the heels of the fleeing Germans left the facility untouched.

After Germany surrendered, the new Avia owners took inventory and found 20 Bf 109G-14s on the verge of completion, along with two Bf 109G-12 trainers. They also found stocks of crated Daimler-Benz DB 605 engines built in Germany and many other parts.

Under the direction of *Ceskoslovenské vojenské letectvo* (the reestablished Czechoslovak Air Force), Avia completed these aircraft. Designated the S 99, the aircraft *was* the advanced Gustav. These were enthusiastically welcomed as the first-line fighter by the *Ceskoslovenské vojenské letectvo* during the uncertain peace following World War II. To top it off, they had come at virtually no cost—much needed by a war-ravaged country with a ruined economy.

Avia then scoured the country, and Hungary and Romania, for all available components of the Messerschmitt fighter. The government ordered these assembled. Not all parts necessary were found in volume, so subcontractors again went to work manufacturing components. The lines geared up for final assembly.

The bottom line: The Bf 109 was back in production!

Avia tooled up for an extended production run, but only 20 were completed before a devastating setback. In September 1945, a sugar refinery at Krasno Bresno burned to the ground. Undoubtedly sabotaged, the refinery had been used to store ammunition—and all the precious DB 605 engines. They were a total loss.

After that, the Czechoslovaks considered their alternatives. They still had the capability to build the Bf 109 airframe. What they needed were powerplants. They found a solution in a large stock of Jumo 211F engines, intended for Heinkel He 111H bombers and also interrupted on assembly lines in Czechoslovakia. The Jumo had comparable power at 1,350 horsepower and, like the Daimler-Benz, it was a liquid-cooled, inverted V-12. All it required was a new cowling, propeller, and spinner for use in the Bf 109.

On engineer's drawings, this looked like a good match. In reality, it wasn't. The Jumo would need a wide-bladed

The Avia S 199 was called the *Mezec*, or Mule, by its contemptuous pilots. It was a Frankenstein monster pieced together mostly from leftover components scavenged after the war. To risk understatement, its performance was substandard. Willy Messerschmitt would not have approved. *Bowers Collection*

The huge paddle blades of the Avia S 199 might have been suitable for a bomber, but not for an agile fighter. The engine of the Avia, the German-built Jumo 211F found in quantity in Czechoslovak warehouses at war's end, had been intended for use in Heinkel He 111H bombers. The Jumo was similar to the Daimler-Benz engine, in that it was a liquid-cooled inverted V-12, but the Jumo called for a blade with large surface area (even the Avia's spinner was narrowed to expose more of the blade). These extra wide blades possibly accounted for the difficulty in synchronization with the cowl guns. Numerous incidents documented by the Israeli Air Force describe the Avia's propeller blades being shot off by the machine's own guns. But that was only one of numerous problems with the Bf 109 airframe coupled with the Jumo 211F, not the least of which was the horrendous handling. *Bowers Collection*

VS 11 propeller—even wider than the Bf 109K. It might be right for an He 111 bomber, but not an agile, single-engined fighter.

The first prototype was ready for flight on March 25, 1947. From the moment the aircraft began to roll down the runway, it was a harrowing experience. Handling characteristics were "appalling." Torque from the three huge paddle blades caused such great twisting and turning during takeoff that the pilot had to fight the rudder, especially after the tailwheel lifted. Landings were even more harrowing, given the ground-looping problems descending from the earliest Messerschmitt design. Worst of all was in between: the flight. The aircraft was sluggish, capricious, and needed constant attention just to maintain straight and level flight. The combination of engine and airframe claimed a top speed of 367 miles per hour, but firsthand reports say it strained to reach 330 or 340 miles per hour in level flight.

Unperturbed, *Ceskoslovenské vojenské letectvo* went ahead with production. It devised armament for the fighter, using what was available—13mm MG 131 cowl-mounted machine guns and the *Rüstsatz 6*—two gondola-mounted 20mm MG 151 cannons under the wings.

Designated the S 199, but unaffectionately called *Mezec* (Mule) by grousing pilots, the Bf 109 mutant was first delivered to Czechoslovak fighter units in February 1948. To expedite production, a second assembly line, in addition to Avia at Cakovice, was established at the Letov factory at Letnany. Between the two, a total of 609 aircraft were built: 129 by Letov and 422 by Avia (58 of them being the two-seat trainer designated CS 199). The S 199 had its own brief and minor evolution. In later production, Avia replaced the framed canopy with a bubble type, updated the radio-transmitter, and modified the landing gear.

The S 199's undistinguished service lasted into the 1950s, when the *Ceskoslovenské vojenské letectvo* unceremoniously pulled it from the inventory.

Israel

Among all the countries desperate to establish some sort of home defense in the war's aftermath, Israel was probably the most desperate. So desperate, in fact, it was willing to buy Czech S 199s.

Before Israel was officially declared an independent state by the United Nations on May 14, 1948, a clandestine military was already forming. This included an air

The Finnish Air Force welcomed the Bf 109s to its first-line fighter units to fight the invading Bolsheviks in early World War II. This aircraft has the wartime Finnish Air Force insignia of a swastika—to Finns a good-luck symbol, suggested in 1918 by a Swedish aristocrat who gave Finland a war-surplus aircraft to start an air force. *Finnish Air Force*

Bf 109Gs of the Swiss Air Force. The Swiss were good and loyal customers of the Bf 109, buying them as early as 1938. The first version to carry Swiss colors was the Dora, and later the Emil in greater numbers. They continued flying Bf 109Gs, seen here in postwar markings, through 1949. *Bowers Collection*

force, hitherto existing only on paper, called *Chel Ha'avir.* In March 1948, one month after the S 199 went into production, *Chel Ha'avir* leaders covertly approached Czechoslovakia for the purchase. They had little choice in "shopping," because sales of arms to the Middle East were forbidden at the time.

The attack from surrounding Arab neighbors was imminent—likely simultaneous with Israel's declaration as a state. With no time to waste, Israel needed arms at any price. The Czechoslovaks needed money as badly as arms, and the Israelis offered American dollars (the United States wouldn't supply arms, but it did supply money). The Israelis struck a deal for 25 S 199s, along with spare

parts and ammunition. Reports of their cost vary widely, anywhere from $50,000 to $190,000 per aircraft. The first 10, delivered on April 23, 1948, were the first combat aircraft of *Chel Ha'avir* to wear the Star of David.

When the inevitable war came, the S 199s saw action alongside new kindred, Spitfires, mostly in ground attack missions. For any former RAF pilot in the vicinity (and there were some in advisor roles), the sight of the two familiar aerodynamic shapes flying in unison must have been a jarring juxtaposition.

The S 199s used in combat were armed the way the Czechoslovaks had built them—with two MG 131 machine guns and two 20mm MG 151 cannons. Aside from the

The Hispano-Aviacion HA-1109-K1L was the sleek-nosed, first version of Spain's Bf 109. It was powered by a 1,300-horsepower Hispano-Suiza 12-Z-89 engine (developed from the French 12Y engine). The aircraft was somewhat underpowered and not ideal as a fighter. *Bowers Collection*

S 199 Specifications

Dimensions—Wingspan: 32 feet, 6 1/2 inches. Length: 29 feet, 6 inches. Height: 8 feet, 6 inches.

Weight—Empty: 5,732 pounds. Gross: 7,716 pounds.

Powerplant—Junkers Jumo 211F inverted V-12, liquid-cooled engine rated at 1,350 horsepower.

Armament—Two wing-mounted 20mm Mauser MG 151 cannons and two 13mm MG 131 machine guns, mounted above the engine in the cowl.

Performance—Maximum speed: 367 miles per hour at 19,700 feet. Range: 528 miles (with 300-liter drop tank). Ceiling: 31,170 feet.

---

handling problems, a major problem quickly became evident in combat: Undependable cowl-gun synchronization with the airscrew. Never a problem in the German version, the S 199 had a penchant for shooting off its own propeller (probably owing to the wide-paddled blades). By the end of the war, only four or five were serviceable, most of the rest being lost to accidents.

Finland

Finland had become a nominal partner in the Axis, joining Germany against Russia three days after the start of Operation *Barbarossa* on June 22, 1941. As such, the *Ilmanvoimien*, or Finnish Air Force, had the opportunity to order Bf 109s, as did Yugoslavia, Bulgaria, Romania, and others.

The first Bf 109s to reach the *Ilmanvoimien* were G-2s. They received many later models of Gustavs as well. The Finns flew them very effectively against their Russian opponents, achieving a superb 12-to-1 kill ratio. Subject to only limited disarmament at war's end, the Finns continued to fly the Gustavs as their front-line fighter.[18] Bf 109Gs numbered as many as 100 in 1948.

Finally phased out by 1954, the same Bf 109s had flown in active Finnish service for 13 years—the longest

continuous operation of authentic Bf 109s in any country, bar none.

Switzerland

The Swiss had known the capabilities of the Bf 109 for a long time. They had ordered early Jumo-equipped Doras during the winter of 1938–39 and ordered 30 Bf 109E-1s when they became available in April 1939. Impressed with the dazzling new fighter, they ordered another 50 Emils. They subsequently ordered a dozen Bf 109Gs.

Being a neutral country, Switzerland finished the war with nearly all these intact. Plus there were a few "strays." Wartime acquisitions included two Bf 109Fs interned after landing at Belp in July 1942, and two Bf 109Gs that landed at Samaden and Affeltraagen in March and December 1944. All four were interned and later folded into the Swiss Air Force.

There were enough Bf 109s to fully outfit five Swiss *Fliegerstaffeln* (much like the Luftwaffe's *Staffeln*). These continued operating until the USAAF declared much of its P-51D fleet surplus in 1948. A gradual transition to Mustangs lasted until December 28, 1949, when the last of the Messerschmitts were withdrawn from active service.

Spain

The Spanish had been the first to know the capabilities of the Bf 109 in firsthand experience. It had dominated Spanish skies during its civil war of the 1930s and, as Germany's *Legion Condor* had received new equipment, the older Bf 109Bs, Cs, and even Es were relegated to Spanish air units. Following the civil war, Spain bought more Emils and also Friedrichs to serve as interceptors in its neutral airspace.

In 1942, Spain's *Ministerio del Aire* sought agreement with Germany's RLM for license to manufacture Bf 109G-2s in Spain. These would be built by Hispano Aviacion. The Spanish version, according to the RLM, was to be designated Bf 109J.

As part of the agreement in early 1943, the Spanish were to receive 25 dismantled G-2s along with the tooling and instruction needed to establish production of their own. The 25 Gustav airframes came, but with little engineering documentation, and no engines, tail assemblies, instruments, armament, or tooling.

The Spaniards waited anxiously but, as the fortunes of war were turning for Germany, either the order fell to low priority or shipping was disrupted. At any rate, it became clear that the rest of the order would not be coming. Tails were easy to fabricate with the tooling and engineering plans they had. The big challenge was an alternate engine to substitute for the DB 605.

The first choice was the Hispano-Suiza 12-Z-89, a 1,300-horsepower V-12. This engine, installed with a VDM airscrew into an older Emil airframe for test purposes, was called HA-1109-J1L. The prototype flew March 2, 1945 with disappointing results.

The Spanish continued flying German-built Bf 109Es and Fs during the search for a compatible homegrown engine for their new fighter. Eventually, the French-built Hispano-Suiza 12-Z-17 engine was installed with better results. The maiden flight of the first prototype was May 1951, and finished production models rolled off assembly lines at Seville in 1952. Designated the HA-1109-K1L, the aircraft impressed no one and was viewed by the *Ejercito del Aire* as more of a single-seat trainer than a combat aircraft, so some were not even armed. Some two-seat trainers were also built with this engine.

In 1953, the *Ejercito del Aire* decided to pursue a new powerplant for its disappointing Bf 109 descendent. A more successful alternative was found for the Gustav airframe: the Rolls-Royce Merlin—the original engine used in the first prototypes 19 years before!

This would be an advanced and more powerful version of the engine, called the Merlin 500-45, which was rated at 1,602 horsepower and used a four-blade Rotol propeller. This marriage of powerplant to airframe was, not surprisingly, successful. Designated the HA-1112-M1L, a German-built airframe was coupled to a British-built engine. (A two-seat trainer was designated HA-1112-M4L.) The aircraft was capable of 419 miles per hour, attained at 13,100 feet.

Since the Merlin was not an inverted V, different cowling was necessary, with exhaust ports high. And there could be no cowl-mounted machine guns, which had characterized Bf 109s from the beginning.

It would be nicknamed the *Buchón* for a more portly nose that, to some, evidently resembled the puffy-chested pigeons that frequented the fountains and squares of Seville. The nose vaguely resembles that of the Merlin-powered Spitfire (especially if the wing root were to be slid aft).

Out of a total of 239 Bf 109s built in Spain, 170 were the Merlin-powered version. Production lasted until 1958, and it remained in the *Ejercito del Aire* combat inventory until spring 1966. This was 32 years after the Bf 109's inception—a span that began in the days of the biplane fighters and ended long after jets were the standard.

In the late 1950s, several years before they would be stricken from the active roles of the *Ejercito del Aire*, the aircraft appeared in Luftwaffe markings for a movie: *The Star of Africa*, the story of Hans-Joachim Marseille. After

HA-1112-M1Ls in formation over Spain. After several miscues coupling powerplants and the Bf 109 airframe, the right combination was found: Ironically, the perfect match was the Rolls-Royce Merlin—the powerplant used in the prototypes of the Bf 109's glory years during the 1930s. With it, the Bf 109 design once again became a very capable propeller-driven aircraft. *Bowers Collection*

it was stricken from the inventory, the famous shape appeared in more movies—most notably *The Battle of Britain*. The movie's producers bought 28 aircraft, including one two-seat trainer, saving them from the smelter. They, in turn, were sold in later years to private individuals and fly today in airshows, as well as in other movies and television shows.

A meager few Daimler-Benz-powered originals still fly (see appendix). They are the vestige that remains of the most produced—and most successful—fighter aircraft of all time.

HA-1112-M1L Specifications

Dimensions—Wingspan: 32 feet, 6 1/2 inches. Length: 29 feet, 10 inches. Height: 8 feet, 6 1/2 inches.

Weight—Empty: 5,855 pounds. Gross: 7,011 pounds.

Powerplant—Rolls-Royce Merlin 500-45 V-12, liquid-cooled engine rated at 1,610 horsepower.

Armament—Two wing-mounted 20mm Hispano HS-404 or HS-808 cannons and eight wing-mounted 80mm Oerlikon rockets.

Performance—Maximum speed: 419 miles per hour at 13,100 feet. Maximum range: 476 miles. Ceiling: 33,450 feet.

END NOTES

[1] *Staffel, Gruppe,* and *Geschwader* were made plural by adding an *n* at the end of each.

[2] The *Staffeln, Gruppen,* and *Geschwadern* designations were altered for Germany's *Legion Condor* in the Spanish Civil War: *Gruppen* were identified as 1.J/88, 2.J/88, and 3.J/88.

[3] They were called "black men" because of their one-piece, black coveralls.

[4] While the M37 was under development, the German Air Ministry was in the process of implementing a new system of aircraft designation. For instance, Heinkel aircraft had the prefix "He," and Focke-Wulf had "Fw." Aircraft produced by Messerschmitt's BFW would have the prefix of Bf followed by its type number. With that new system, the M 37 became the Bf 108. Compounding the confusion that lasts to this day, Messerschmitt's aircraft for a time carried the prefix of "Me" before type number. That's why the famous fighter is known by both "Bf 109" and "Me 109."

[5] Translated into English in *Willy Messerschmitt* by Frank Vann.

[6] Facilities here would be inadequate for the mass production needed in the years to come. While a new factory, complete with adjacent runway, was being built at Regensburg to replace it, other German companies were contracted to build the Messerschmitt fighter's B version (and the C and D versions to come). These included the Erla Maschinenwerk at Leipzig, Focke-Wulf at Bremen, and Gerhard Fieseler Werke at Kassel. An Austrian builder, Wiener-Neustadter-Flugseugwerke, was contracted later. Bf 109s would also eventually be built in Czechoslovakia, Hungary, and Romania.

[7] Varying propeller pitch, along with throttle, caused a continuous rising and falling of engine rpm. As Bf 109s flew over Great Britain during the Battle of Britain, the people could tell which fighters were RAF and which were German, because the sound of the German engine always seemed to be rising and falling, whereas the sound of the RAF fighters didn't fluctuate so.

[8] During the battle of Poland, the RAF flew two missions against the German Navy. There had been no direct attack against Germany itself, but RAF raids targeted the German fleet on September 4 and 28, 1939. British Blenheim and Wellington bombers penetrated German air space over the German Bight to attack the capital ships. On the first raid, the bombers were confronted by the Bf 109s of II/JG 77, whose pilots scored their first victories against the RAF, downing two Wellingtons in the morning and a Blenheim later in the afternoon. Flak brought other RAF aircraft down.

[9] The reports somewhat *over*estimated the RAF's existing fighter strength while considerably *under*estimating production capabilities for turning out new fighters.

[10] Luftwaffe pilots also reported gross exaggerations, which in turn were even more puffed out of shape by German propaganda.

[11] There is confusion about exactly *when* the Battle of Britain began. A few German sources hardly acknowledge that the Battle of Britain, as an event, ever happened. What they recognize is *Adlerangriff* that began on *Adlertag*. Others recognize the Battle of Britain, but not beginning August 8, 1940, as did the RAF. Still attacking only targets at sea and not on English soil that day, the Luftwaffe saw no distinction in the event to mark the beginning of the Battle of Britain. Germans generally view the start as August 13, when land targets were attacked in force.

[12] Erwin Frey later became Erich Hartmann's crew chief and at war's end went with Hartmann to a prison camp in Russia.

[13] This overheating and consequent fire were believed to have forced Hans-Joachim Marseille's bailout from a new G-2, causing his death when he was struck by the tail.

[14] Translated in Armand van Ishoven's *Messerschmitt Bf 109 at War.*

[15] Albert Speer became responsible for aircraft production after Erhard Milch. Milch had more or less wrestled control of it from Ernst Udet, who committed suicide in November 15, 1941.

[16] The first had been November 29, 1942. Ilfrey recounted that "Both my flight leader and I got a Messerschmitt 110. That was the day 12 of us lined abreast and flew through, blasting everything in our path. Only 6 of us came out without bad battle damage." Journalist Ernie Pyle mentions this mission and Ilfrey's other victories to date in his book, *Here Is Your War* (1943). In a glowing vignette, Pyle describes Jack Ilfrey as "a fine person and more or less typical of all boys who flew our deadly fighters. . . . It was hard to conceive of his ever having killed anybody, for . . . his face was good-humored, his darkish hair was childishly uncontrollable and popped up into a little curlicue at the front of his head." Pyle expresses his own opinion about P-38s versus Bf 109s by noting: "If two Lightnings and two Messerschmitt 109s got into a fight, the Americans were almost bound to come out the little end of the horn . . ." It was an assessment hotly contested by P-38 pilots!

[17] Bader became a fighter pilot after graduating from the Royal Air Force Flying School in 1930, then lost both his legs in a flying accident in December 1931. He argued his way back into service and served as commander of 242 Squadron during the Battle of Britain, and subsequently was appointed commander of 11 Wing at Tangmere. Over Belgium, he crashed after colliding with a German plane on August 9, 1941, and spent the rest of the war as a POW.

[18] The Finns were allowed to keep only 60 military aircraft active in the treaty signed at war's end with Russia. They had a half-dozen other fighter types obtained from various countries and scrapped them all, choosing to keep a fleet of Bf 109G-2s, G-6s, and G-14s.

BIBLIOGRAPHY

Ackerman, Robert W. *The Maintenance of Army Aircraft in the United States 1939–1945*. USAAF Historical Study No. 88, 1954.

Bader, Douglas. *Fight for the Sky: The Story of the Spitfire and Hurricane*. London: Sidgwick & Jackson, 1990.

Beaman, John R. Jr., and Jerry L. Campbell. *Messerschmitt Bf 109 in Action*, Part 1. Carrollton, Texas: Squadron/Signal Publications, Inc., 1980.

Bekker, Cajus. *The Luftwaffe War Diaries*. London: McDonald & Co. Ltd., 1966.

Bergstrom, Dennis D. *Gallant Warriors: Propeller-Driven Warbird Fighter and Bomber Survivors Around the World*. Spokane, Washington, self-published, 1994.

Bickers, Richard Townshend. *The Battle of Britain*. New York: Prentice Hall Press, 1990.

Caidin, Martin. *Me 109: Willy Messerschmitt's Peerless Fighter*. New York: Ballantine Books Inc., 1972.

Constable, Trevor J., and Colonel Raymond F. Toliver. *Horrido!* New York: The MacMillan Company, 1968.

Craig, James F. *The Messerschmitt Bf.109*. New York: Arco Publishing Company, Inc., 1968.

Deighton, Len. *Fighter: The True Story of the Battle of Britain*. New York: Harper Paperbacks, 1994.

Ethell, Jeffrey L., and Steve Pace. *Spitfire*. Osceola, Wisconsin: MBI Publishing Co., 1997.

Galland, Adolf. *The First and the Last: The German Fighter Force in World War II*. London: Methuen Publishing Limited, 1955.

Green, William. *Augsburg Eagle: The Story of the Messerschmitt 109*. New York: Doubleday and Company, Inc., 1971.

Held, Werner. *Fighter!* Englewood Cliffs, NJ: Prentice-Hall, Inc., 1979.

Ilfrey, Jack, and Max Reynolds. *Happy Jack's Go-Buggy: A World War II Fighter Pilot's Personal Document*. Hicksville, New York: Exposition Press, 1979.

Jablonski, Edward. *Terror from the Sky*. New York: Doubleday & Company, Inc., 1971.

Johnson, J. E. *Wing Leader*. New York: Ballantine Books Inc., 1956.

Knoke, Heinz. *I Flew for the Führer*. London: Greenhill Books, 1997.

Lande, D. A. *From Somewhere in England*. Osceola, Wisconsin: MBI Publishing Co., 1990.

Lay, Beirne. "The Great Regensburg Raid" from *The Saturday Evening Post* anthology, *Battle: True Stories of Combat in World War II*. New York: Curtis Publishing Company, 1965.

Lerche, Hans-Werner. *Luftwaffe Test Pilot*. New York and London: Jane's Information Group Ltd., 1980.

Nowarra, Heinz J. *The Messerschmitt 109: A Famous German Fighter*. Los Angeles: Aero Publishers, Inc., 1963.

Payne, Michael. *Messerschmitt Bf 109 in the West, 1937–1940*. London: Greenhill Books, 1998.

Pyle, Ernie. *Here Is Your War*. New York: Henry Holt and Company, 1943.

Quill, Jeffrey. *Spitfire: A Test Pilot's Story*. Manchester, England: Crécy Publishing Limited, 1998.

Royal Aircraft Establishment (RAE). *Flying Characteristics of Messerschmitt Aircraft*, Translation No. 99, August 1946.

Scutts, Jerry. *Messerschmitt Bf 109: The Operational Record*. Osceola, Wisconsin: MBI Publishing Co., 1996.

Steinhilper, Ulrich, and Peter Osborne. *Spitfire on My Tail: A View from the Other Side*. Kent, England: Independent Books, 1989.

Townsend, Peter. *Duel of Eagles*. New York: Simon and Schuster, 1970.

United States Army Air Forces. *Aircraft Evaluation Report: German Messerschmitt 109F*, July 1943.

United States Army Air Forces. *Foreign Aircraft Report No. 101*, November 1940.

Van Ishoven, Armand. *Messerschmitt Bf 109 at War*. Hersham, England: Ian Allen Ltd., 1977.

Vann, Frank. *Willy Messerschmitt*. Somerset, England: Patrick Stephens Limited, 1993.

Zobel, Fritz X., and Jakob Maria Mathmann. *Messerschmitt Bf 109*, Volume 2. Atglen, Pennsylvania: Schiffer Military History, 1996.

APPENDICES

SPECIFICATIONS

Bf 109 Version	Engine	Takeoff Hp	Speed Max.	Altitude at Max. Speed	Ceiling Feet	Armament
B-1	Jumo 201Da	635	292	13,100	29,500	Two MG 17
B-2	Jumo 210E/G	640/670	298	13,100	31,200	Two MG 17
C-1	Jumo 210Ga	700	292	14,765	31,200	Four MG 17
C-2	Jumo 210Ga	700	292	14,765	31,200	Five MG 17
C-3	Jumo 210Ga	700	292	14,765	29,800	Four MG 17, one MG FF
D	DB 600Aa	960	357	11,480	34,500	Two MG 17, one MG FF
E-1	DB 601A	1,100	342	13,210	34,500	Two MG 17, two MG FF (or four MG 17)
E-2	DB 601A	1,100	342	13,210	34,500	Two MG 17, three MG FF
E-3	DB 601Aa	1,100	348	19,700	36,000	Two MG 17, three MG FF
E-4	DB 601Aa	1,100	357	19,700	36,000	Two MG 17, two MG FF
E-4/Trop	DB 601Aa	1,100	357	19,700	36,000	Two MG 17, two MG FF
E-4/N	DB 601N	1,200	373	19,700	32,800	Two MG 17, two MG FF; One 250-kg or four 50-kg bombs
E-4/B	DB 601Aa	1,100	357	19,700	32,800	Two MG 17, two MG FF; One 250-kg or four 50-kg bombs
E-5	DB 601Aa	1,100	357	19,700	32,800	Two MG 17
E-5/Trop	DB 601Aa	1,100	357	19,700	32,800	Two MG 17
E-6	DB 601N	1,200	373	19,700	36,000	Two MG 17, two MG FF
E-7	DB 601N	1,200	366	19,700	36,000	Two MG 17, two MG FF
E-8	DB 601E	1,300	366	19,700	32,800	Two MG 17, two MG FF
E-9	DB 601E	1,300	378	19,700	32,800	Two MG 17
T	DB 601N	1,200	357	19,700	34,500	Two MG 17, two MG FF
F-1	DB 601N	1,200	369	19,700	36,090	Two MG 17, one MG FF
F-2	DB 601N	1,200	366	19,700	36,090	Two MG 17, one MG 151/15
F-2/Trop	DB 601N	1,200	366	19,700	36,090	Two MG 17, one MG 151/15
F-3	DB 601E	1,300	388	21,325	39,400	Two MG 17, one MG 151/15
F-4	DB 601E	1,300	388	21,325	39,400	Two MG 17, one MG 151/20
F-4/Trop	DB 601E	1,300	388	21,325	39,400	Two MG 17, one MG 151/15
F-4/B	DB 601E	1,300	341	19,700	36,000	Two MG 17, one MG 151/15; One 250-kg or four 50-kg bombs
F-5	DB 601E	1,300	373	19,700	39,400	Two MG 17
F-6	DB 601E	1,300	373	19,700	39,400	None
G-1 (P)	DB 605A	1,475	398	20,670	39,700	Two MG 17, one MG 151/20
G-1/Trop (P)	DB 605A	1,475	398	20,670	39,700	Two MG 131, one MG 151/20

Bf 109 Version	Engine	Takeoff Hp	Speed Max.	Altitude at Max. Speed	Ceiling Feet	Armament
G-2	DB 605A	1,475	398	20,670	39,700	Four MG 17
G-3 (P)	DB 605A	1,475	398	20,670	39,700	Two MG 17, one MG 151/20
G-4	DB 605A	1,475	398	20,670	39,700	Two MG 17
G-5 (P)	DB 605D	1,450	386	22,640	37,900	Two MG 131, one MG 151/20
G-6	DB 605D	1,450	386	22,640	37,900	Two MG 131, three MG 151/20
G-8	*	1,450	386	22,640	41,400	One Mk. 108
G-10	DB 605D	1,450	426	24,280	41,400	Two MG 131, one Mk. 108
G-12	DB 605A	1,475	398	20,670	39,700	None or one Mk. 108
G-14	*	1,475	404	19,700	41,400	Two MG 131, one MG 151/20
H	*	1,450	–	–	–	One Mk. 108
K-2	DB 605ASCM	1,475	452	19,700	41,000	One 30mm Mk. 103 or Mk. 108; Two MG 151/15
K-4 (P)	DB 605ASCM	1,475	452	19,700	41,000	One 30mm Mk. 103 or Mk. 108; Two MG 151/15

*Optional engines: Daimler-Benz DB 605AM, AS, ASB, ASM, or ASD
(P) Indicates pressurized cockpit.

FOREIGN MANUFACTURE

Version	Engine	Takeoff Hp	Speed Max.	Altitude at Max. Speed	Ceiling Feet	Range Miles	Armament
Spanish-built Bf 109 variant							
HA-1112-M1L	RR Merlin	1,610	419	13,100	33,450	476	Two HS 404 or 408
HA-1112-M4L	RR Merlin	1,610	413	13,100	32,800	472	None (trainer)
Czechoslovakian-built Bf 109 variant							
S 99	DB 605A	1,475	375	–	32,800	–	Two MG 151, Two MG 131
S 199	Jumo 211F	1,300	367	19,700	31,170	528	Two MG 151, Two MG 131
CS 199	Jumo 211F	1,300	–	–	–	–	None (trainer)

SURVIVING AIRCRAFT

Aircraft Produced	Total	Flying condition	Restorations under way	Status unknown	Museum Display	Total Surviving
Bf 109	33,000	1	3	6	15	25
HA-1110-K1L	N/A	0	0	1	0	1
HA-1112-K1L	N/A	0	0	0	1	1
HA-1112-M1L	N/A	4	6	9	11	30
S 199	N/A	0	0	0	1	1
CS 199	N/A	0	0	0	2	2

Aircraft	Military ID	Former reg.	Source	Owner	City, State, or Country	Current Markings	Status
Bf 109B-2	1010	V10, D-IAKO		Obserschleisseim	Munich, Germany	Derelict hulk	M
Bf 109E		Legion Condor.	6-88	Robert Lamplough	North Weald, England		S
Bf 109E	3535		Russia, 1994	Ed & Rose Zalesky	Surrey, BC, Canada		S
Bf 109E	1983				Germany (being restored in UK)		R
Bf 109E-3	1289	II/JG 26, Black 2 SH+FA		S. African Museum of Military History	Johannesburg	Displayed in crashed condition	M
Bf 109E-3	1342	4./JG 51	France	Flying Heritage Coll.	Bellevue, Washington		R
Bf 109E-3	1407	2./JG 77, Black 8	From lake, 1993	Hungary			S
Bf 109E-3	4101	2./JG 51, Black 12		RAF Museum	Hendon, England		M
Bf 109E-3	2242	Swiss AF: J-355	Swiss AF	Swiss Transport Museum	Lucerne, Switzerland	Swiss Air Force	M
Bf 109E-3	790	Legion Condor: 6-106, 2/J88, Span. AF: 6-106		Deutsches Museum	Munich, Germany	AJ+YM, Wkr 2804	M
Bf 109E-6	1190	II/JG 26, White 4		Imperial War Museum	Duxford, England	White 4	R
Bf 109E-7	3579	4./JG 5, White 7		Museum of Flying	Santa Monica, California	White 14	F
Bf 109E-7	5975		Russia	Warbird Recovery	Broomfield, Colorado		R
Bf 109F-1				Ailes Aniennes Marsei	Vinon-sur-Verdon, France		M
Bf 109F-2	31010	I/JG 27, White 6		S. African Museum of Military History	Johannesburg	I/JG 27 White 6	M
Bf 109F-4	10132	Stab II/JG54		Canadian National Air Museum	Rockcliffe, Ontario	Grey-green camo	M
Bf 109F-4	10144	Norwegian Air Force	Russia, 1994	Warbird Recovery	Broomfield, Colorado		R

Aircraft	Military ID	Former reg.	Source	Owner	City, State, or Country	Current Markings	Status
Bf 109F-4	10212		Russia	Warbird Recovery	Broomfield, Colorado		R
Bf 109F-4	10256		Russia	Warbird Recovery	Broomfield, Colorado		R
Bf 109F-4	10270		Russia	Warbird Recovery	Broomfield, Colorado		R
Bf 109F-4	7585			Charleston Aviation	Essex, England		S
Bf 109F-4	7108	NE + ML	Finland	Aviation Museum of Central Finland	Tikkakoski, Finland		S
Bf 109F-4	8147	6./JG 54, Yellow 8	Russia, 1992	Charleston Aviation	West Sussex, England		S
Bf 109F-4	8993		Russia, 1998	Jim Pearce	Shoreham, England		S
Bf 109G			Russia, 1994	Ben Kolotilin	Atlanta, Georgia		S
Bf 109G			Russia, 1994	Ben Kolotilin	Atlanta, Georgia		S
Bf 109G			Russia, 1994	Ed & Rose Zalesky	Surrey, BC, Canada		S
Bf 109G-1	14141	2./JG 5, Black 6		Flyhistorisk Museum	Sola AFB, Norway		R
Bf 109G-2				Luftfahrt Museum	Hannover, Germany		M
Bf 109G-2/Trop	10639	8478M, RN228		Imperial War Museum	Duxford, England	Black 6 desert camouflage	S
Bf 109G-2	14798	Black 1	Russia, 1992	David Price	Santa Monica, California		S
Bf 109G-2	15458			Charleston Aviation	Essex, England		S
Bf 109G-4	19310	2./JG 52, White 3		Jeet Mahal	Canada	Regia Aeronautica 364-5	M
Bf 109G-5	15343			Vliegend Museum Seepe	Breda, Holland		M
Bf 109G-6			Lake Swilbo	David Prewitt & C. Kelly	Melbourne, Australia		S
Bf 109G-6	14792	Yugoslav AF: 9663	Yugoslav AF	Yugoslavian AF Museum	Belgrade, Yugoslavia		M
Bf 109G-6	160163	USAAF: FE-496/T2-496		National Air & Space	Washington, DC	White 2	M
Bf 109G-6	165227	Finnish AF: MT-452	Finnish AF	Suomen Ilmailumusei	Utti AFB, Finland		M

Aircraft	Military ID	Former reg.	Source	Owner	City, State, or Country	Current Markings	Status
Bf 109G-6	167271	Finish AF: MT-507	Finnish AF	Aviation Museum of Central Finland	Tikkakoski, Finland		M
Bf 109G-10/U4	610824	Bulgarian AF, Yugoslav AF: 9664		USAF Museum	Dayton, Ohio	Blue 4	M
Bf 109G-10/U4	610937	USAAF: FE124/T2-124	USAF	Evergreen Vintage Aircraft Museum	McMinnville, Oregon	Erich Hartmann markings	F
Bf 109G-10	611943	Yellow 13, USAAF: FE-122/Te-122	USAF	Planes of Fame	Chino, California	Yellow 13	M
Bf 109G-14	163824			Australian War Museum	Canberra, Australia		M
Bf 109G-14	784993	JG 53, White 13		Raymond Wagner	Saarlouis, Germany		M
Bf 209V-1	1185			Muz. Lotnictwa I Astro	Krokov, Poland	Fuselage	M

Foreign Manufacture

Aircraft	Military ID	Former reg.	Source	Owner	City, State, or Country	Current Markings	Status
				Czechoslovakan-built Bf 109 variant			
Avia S 199	199178	Czech AF: UF-25	Czech AF	Vojenske Museum	Prague, Czech Republic		M
Avia CS 199	199565	Czech AF: UF-26	Czech AF	Vojenske Museum	Prague, Czech Republic		M
Avia CS 199	782358	Czech AF, Israeli AF	Israeli AF	Israeli AF Museum	Hazerim AB, Israel	112-T	M
				Spanish-built Bf 109 variant			
HA-1110-K1L	40-2	Spanish AF: C4K-112, G-AWHC		Wilson C. Edwards	Big Spring, Texas		S
HA-1112-K1L	46	Spanish AF: C.4J-10		Museo del Aire	Madrid, Spain	94-28	M

Aircraft	Military ID	Former reg.	Owner	City, State, or Country	Current Markings	Status
HA-1112-M1L		Spanish AF: C.4K-?	Luftwaffen Museum	Germany	Luftwaffe scheme	M
HA-1112-M1L		Spanish AF: C.4K-?	New England Air Museum	Windsor Locks, Connecticut		M
HA-1112-M1L		Spanish AF: C.4K-156	Musee de l'Air	Paris/Le Bourget, France	Spanish AF: C.4K-156, 471-28	M
HA-1112-M1L**		Spanish AF: C.4K-64	USAF Museum	Dayton, Ohio		M
HA-1112-M1L**		Spanish AF: C.4K-162	Rene Meyer	Paris, France		R
HA-1112-M1L		N6109	Robert Murphy	Quantico, Virginia		S
HA-1112-M1L**	139	Spanish AF: C4K-75, G-AWHG, N3109G	R. Bastet	La Ferte-Alais, France		R
HA-1112-M1L	145	Spanish AF: C4K-105, G-AWHH	Jim Porter	Batavia, Illinois		S
HA-1112-M1L	166	Spanish AF: C4K-106, G-AWHI	Wilson C. Edwards	Big Spring, Texas		S
HA-1112-M1L	170	Spanish AF: C4K-107, G-AWHS N170BG	Old Flying Machine Co.	Duxford, England	Red 3, yellow nose, camo	S
HA-1112-M1L	171	Spanish AF: C.4K-100, G-AWHJ, N90605	Kalamazoo Air Zoo	Kalamazoo, Michigan	"Hapi" C.4K-19, Blue	M
HA-1112-M1L	172	Spanish AF: C4K-102, G-AWHK, N9938	Real Airplane Co.	Breighton, England	(ex-CAF)	R
HA-1112-M1L**	178	Spanish AF: C4K-121	William C. Anderson	Geneseo, New York		R
HA-1112-M1L	183	Spanish AF: C4K-114	West Canada Aviation Museum	Winnipeg, Canada	Spanish AF: C.4K-114, 471-39	M
HA-1112-M1L~	186	Spanish AF: C.4K-122, G-AWHL, N109J	Champlin Fighter Mus	Mesa, Arizona	Yellow nose	M
HA-1112-M1L	187	Spanish AF: C4K-99, G-AWHM	Wilson C. Edwards	Big Spring, Texas		S
HA-1112-M1L	190	Spanish AF: C4K-126, G-AWHD	Wilson C. Edwards	Big Spring, Texas		S
HA-1112-M1L	193	Spanish AF: C4K-130, G-AWHN	Jack Erickson	Tillamook, Oregon	Luftwaffe camo	R
HA-1112-M1L	194	Spanish AF: C.4K-134	Wittmundhafen AFB	Germany		M
HA-1112-M1L**	195	Spanish AF: C4K-135	MBB Aircraft	Manching, Germany	FM-BB	S

Aircraft	Military ID	Former reg.	Owner	City, State, or Country	Current Markings	Status
HA-1112-M1L	199	Spanish AF: C.4K-127, G-AWHO, N90601, N109BF	EAA Aviation Museum	Oshkosh, Wisconsin		M
HA-1112-M1L	201	Spanish AF: C4K-131	Eric Vormezeele	Braaschaat, Belgium	Luftwaffe 1	F
HA-1112-M1L**	213	Spanish AF: C4K-40?, D-FEHD	Hans Dittes	Mannheim, Germany	Black 2	F
HA-1112-M1L	220	Spanish AF: C4K-152, G-AWHR	Wilson C. Edwards	Big Spring, Texas		S
HA-1112-M1L	226	Spanish AF: C.4K-158	Museo del Aire	Madrid, Spain	471-23	M
HA-1112-M1L	228	Spanish AF: C.4K-170, G-AWHS	Teknikmuseum Speyer	Sinsheim, Germany	Luftwaffe 4	M
HA-1112-M1L	234	Spanish AF: C4K-169, G-AWHT, N9939	Harold Kindsvater	Clovis, California		R
HA-1112-M1L	235	Spanish AF: C4K-172, N48157, G-BJZZ G-HUNN	Jim Cavanaugh	Addison, Texas	Luftwaffe camo (Galland)	F
HA-1112-M1L	557	Spanish AF: C4K-?, N109DW	Planes of Fame	Chino, California	Yellow 5	F
HA-1112-M1L	67	Spanish AF: C4K-31, G-AWHE	Confederate Air Force	Midland, Texas	14, 100 on tail	S

**Restored as G version with DB 605 engine

~Restored as E version with DB 601 engine

F = Flyable

R = Being restored

S = Stored or staus unknown

M = Museum/display

Source: *Gallant Warriors* (eighth edition, January 2000) by Dennis Bergstrom.

INDEX

Adlerangriff, 54–57, 59, 62

Adlertag, 56, 59

Amiot 143, 49, 51

Ar 80V-2, 12

Arado, 8, 10, 12

B-17 Flying Fortress, 47, 96, 101

B-24 Liberator, 96

Bader, Douglas, 55, 107, 108

Barkorn, Gerhard, 103

Battle of Britain, 17, 18, 28, 29, 53, 55, 59, 60, 63, 70, 102

Battle of France, 29, 52, 53

Battle of Heglioland Bight, 49

Battle of Kursk, 95

Battle of the Bulge, 103

Bell P-39 Airacobra, 92

Bf 108, 10, 12, 84

Bf 109 cockpit, 45

Bf 109, 10, 12, 14, 17–20, 30, 31, 34, 41, 43, 44, 47, 49, 50, 52–54, 56, 57, 59–61, 67, 68, 78, 86–88, 93, 95, 99, 101, 103, 112–114

Bf 109, 9

Bf 109A, 21

Bf 109B, 16

Bf 109B, 17

Bf 109B-1, 18, 21, 30

Bf 109B-2, 18, 19, 21, 22

Bf 109C, 20, 23

Bf 109C-1, 22

Bf 109C-2, 22

Bf 109C-3, 22

Bf 109D, 23, 26

Bf 109E, 18, 35, 49, 50, 55, 56, 60, 61, 69, 87, 88, 90, 116

Bf 109E-1, 26, 29

Bf 109E-2, 26, 28

Bf 109E-3, 26, 28, 29, 34, 35, 50, 51, 53, 62, 63, 70, 90

Bf 109E-4, 16, 17, 24–26, 28, 29, 33, 53, 63, 70

Bf 109E-4/B, specifications, 29

Bf 109E-4/N specifications, 71

Bf 109E-4/Trop, 36

Bf 109E-5, 70, 71

Bf 109E-6, 71

Bf 109E-7, 72

Bf 109E-8, 72. 73

Bf 109E-9, 72, 73

Bf 109F, 64, 74–76, 88, 116

Bf 109G diagram, 80, 81

Bf 109G, 64, 76–79, 82–85, 90, 95, 116, 117

Bf 109J, 116

Bf 109K, 70, 83, 85

Bf 109T-1, 74

Bf 109T-2, 73

Bf 109V-1, 11, 15

Bf 109V-14, 23, 26

Bf 109V-15, 26

Bf 109V-17, 26

Bf 109V-2, 12

Bf 109V-3, 8, 14

Bf 109V-4, 14, 19

Bf 109V-7, 21

Bf 109V-8, 19

Bf 110, 49, 53, 55, 58, 59, 87, 101

Bf 110C-4B, 29

BFW, 9–11

Blitzkrieg, 51, 55, 70

Bretnutz, Heinz, 93

Churchill, Winston, 53, 54, 60, 90

Daimler Benz 601, 18, 23, 34, 60, 77

Daimler Benz 601E, 63, 72

Daimler Benz 601N, 71

Daimler Benz 605, 77, 82, 113, 117

Daimler Benz 605D, 47

Deichmann, Paul, 57

Farman 222, 49

Fliegerkorps, 6

Fliegerstaffeln, 116

Flugzeugbau, 9

Focke-Wulf, 8, 10, 12, 77, 96

Franco, Francisco, 16, 18, 19

Fw 159V2, 12

Fw 190, 68, 77, 84, 98, 99, 101

Galland, Adolf, 13, 16, 18, 59, 60, 67, 86, 90, 101–103

Gerhard, Dieter, 69

Geschwader, 6

Gladiator interceptor, 87

Göring, Hermann, 8, 10, 16, 51, 52, 54–56, 63, 86, 93, 101, 103

Gruppen, 6, 29

Gunter, Siegried, 12

Gunter, Walter, 12

HA-1109-K1L, 117

HA-1112-M1L specifications, 117

Harder, Jürgen, 90

Harris, Sir Arthur, 96

Harrison, Bill, 110, 111

Hartmann, Eric, 6, 103

He 111, 23, 31, 41, 112, 114

He 112V-1, 12, 14

He 112V-3, 14

He 51, 17, 18, 22, 58

Heemsoth, Richard, 101

Heinkel 111, 87

Heinkel He 45, 9

Heinkel He 51, 8

Heinkel He 51, 8, 11

Heinkel, 8, 10, 12–14, 23

Heinkel, Ernst, 9

Henschel Hs 123, 31

Hitler, Adolf, 16, 30, 51–55, 59, 63, 70, 88, 90–98, 101, 103

Hurricane, 52, 54, 55, 58, 87, 88, 91, 107, 108

Ilfrey, Jack, 105–107

Jagdfliegerschulen, 49

Jagdgeschwader, 6, 16, 50, 53, 63

Jagdgruppe, 18

Jodl, Alfred, 112

Johnson, J.E., 20

Jumo 210, 8, 11, 12, 23

Jumo 210Da, 21

Jumo 210E, 21, 22

Jumo 210G, 22

Kanalkrankheit, 57

Kesselring, Albert, 31

Kestrel V-12, 11

Knoetsch, Hans, 11, 12

Knoke, Heinz, 59, 68, 69, 77

Layrargues, Pommier, 52

Legion Condor, 17–20, 22, 30, 49, 116

Lerche, Hans-Werner, 64, 65

Löhr, Alexander, 31

Luftwaffe, 6, 8, 10, 11, 14, 16, 18, 21, 28, 29, 31, 32, 34, 49–56, 59, 63, 64, 68, 77, 83, 86, 88, 90–97, 99, 101, 103, 105, 106, 112, 117

Lusser, Robert, 10

Marseille, Hans-Joachim, 37, 87, 89, 102, 117

Me 109, 16, 19, 26, 28, 97

Merlin XII, 63

Messerschmitt 262 jet fighter, 97

Messserschmitt, Willy, 8–14, 19, 20, 23, 32, 52, 58

Milch, Erhard, 8–10, 87

Mistrel, 84

Mölders, Werner, 52, 53, 62, 70, 86, 93, 102

Mussolini, Benito, 90

Normandy invasion, 103

Oberleutnant, 6

Oberst, 6

Oberstleutnant, 6

Oesau, Walter, 93

Oest, Werner, 67, 68

Operation *Barbarossa*, 17, 86, 90, 94, 95

Operation *Battleaxe*, 88

Operation *Beethoven*, 84

Operation *Crusader*, 88, 89

Operation *Seelöwe*, 55, 86

Operation *Torch*, 90

Osterkamp, Theo, 62

P-38 Lightning, 99

P-47 Thunderbolt, 99

P-51 Mustang, 44, 77, 99, 101, 103, 110

Paulus, Friedrich, 95

Polikarpov I-15, 17

Polikarpov I-16, 17

Quill, Jeffrey, 104, 105

RAF, 41, 50, 52, 53, 55, 56, 58, 59, 61, 68, 70, 79, 86–90, 90, 91, 96, 101, 115

Rall, Günther, 5, 103

Red Baron, 17, 93

Rethel, Walter, 10

Richthofen, Manfred von, 17, 55, 59, 93

Rolls-Royce Merlin engine, 48

Rommel, 86–88, 90, 105

Rotte, 6, 20, 60, 65

S 199 Specifications, 116

Schellmann, Wolfgang, 93, 102

Schwarm, 6, 20, 54

Sherman, Dennis, 42, 108–110

Spanish Civil War, 8, 16, 17, 30, 53, 60, 90, 92

Spitfire Mk.V, 90

Spitfire, 11, 52, 54–56, 59, 61, 63–65, 68–70, 77, 96, 103, 104, 107, 108, 115

Staffel, 6, 17, 18, 35, 59, 78

Staffelkapitan, 6

Steinhilper, Ulrich, 26, 57, 65–67

Stoll, Wilhelm, 67, 69

Taifun, 8, 10, 12

Thunderbolt, 103

Tomahawk, 88

Udet, Ernst, 10, 13, 20

USAAF, 70, 79, 96, 99, 103, 116

Vann, Frank, 10

Wimmer, Wilhelm, 10

World War I, 10, 12, 13, 16, 17, 59, 93

World War II, 15, 19, 31, 52, 70, 108, 110–112

Wurster, Herman, 14